The Future of North-South Relations

Towards Sustainable Economic and Social Development

Publisher's Note

The books published in the *Forward Studies Series* contain a selection of research studies, reports, seminar or conference proceedings of the European Commission's Forward Studies Unit.

In publishing these works in the *Forward Studies Series*, the original material has undergone editorial rearrangement. Bibliographies have been added where necessary.

Forward Studies Series

THE FUTURE OF NORTH-SOUTH RELATIONS

Towards Sustainable Economic and Social Development

Foreword by Jacques Santer

St. Martin's Press
New York

Office for Official Publications
of the European Communities

THE FUTURE OF NORTH-SOUTH RELATIONS

St. Martin's Press, Scholarly and Reference Division,
175 Fifth Avenue, New York, N.Y. 10010

First published in the United States of America in 1998

Printed in Great Britain

ISBN: 0-312-21601-7

Library of Congress Cataloging-in-Publication Data

The future of North-South relations : towards sustainable economic and
  social development / Forward Studies Unit at the European Commission.
      p.   cm. – (Forward studies series)
  Includes bibliographical references.
  ISBN 0-312-21601-7 (cloth)
  1. International economic relations. 2. Sustainable development.
  3. Economic development–Social aspects. 4. Economic forecasting.
  5. European Union countries–Foreign economic relations–Developing
  countries. 6. Developing countries–Foreign economic relations-
  -European Union countries. I. European Commission. Forward Studies
  Unit. II. Series.
  HF 1359.F88   1998
  337–DC21   98–17450
                                                                    CIP

Contents

Annexes

Foreword

Although much of Europe's time and energy seem to be taken up at the moment with the internal challenges it has to face, it cannot afford to think of itself as an island of stability in a world in disarray.

That is why I am glad that first of the Forward Studies Series is devoted to exploring the European view of the future of North-South relations, after the tremendous upheaval which followed the ending of the Cold War. That great turn in events, symbolized by the fall of the Berlin Wall, not only brought about a drastic reshaping of European geopolitics, it also opened up a new era in world relations.

This publication prescribes no particular course of action. It sets out ways forward which will potentially clarify the tasks that are bound for a long time to be on the agenda of an international community, a community which is still proving slow to form itself and to which Europe has its own experience to offer and its own contribution to make.

I believe three messages come over loud and clear in the report.

The first is how important it is to carry out a global overhaul and renewal of the multilateral world economic order, in terms of both effectiveness and legitimacy. This is the new trade-off the North owes the South. As far as the countries of the South are concerned, the end of East-West confrontation now creates an obligation to apply the rules of good governance.

The second is that we must stress the benefits to Europe of maintaining a comprehensive development cooperation policy which goes beyond the economic and financial spheres to encompass science, technology, social development and the environment.

Thirdly and lastly, the book emphasizes how useful a tool development contracts can be in incorporating the rights and duties of a variety of players into a relationship of mutual respect.

This publication will also help people in Europe work out the changes that have still to be made in their relations with the countries of the South to take account of the new worldwide context. The ideas in it have already provided the Commission with food for thought about the current reforms of the United Nations, the development of relations between the European Union and the ACP countries and the search for a way of fostering sustainable development in Europe which is consistent with the defence of its interests on the world stage. They have also been heard in international think-tanks such as the Commission on global governance co-chaired by Ingvar Carlsson and Sridath Ramphal.

Jacques Santer
President of the European Commission

'Le réel est étroit
le possible est immense'

Lamartine

Introduction

The European Commission mandated the Forward Studies
Unit on 27 November 1991 to establish a report on the
prospects of North-South relations (see mandate in Annex 3).
In accordance with this mandate, the report concentrates on the
analysis of the evolution of North-South interdependencies in a
changing geopolitical situation and attempts to outline the
parameters of a global strategy to avoid the risks resulting from a
mishandling of these interdependencies on the basis of
common concepts of good governance and global governance
for the promotion of sustainable social and economic development. The report further formulates strategic priorities for the
Community in contributing to a more coherent global
approach, in line with its specific geopolitical interests and an
adequate internal division of tasks. However, the report does
not contain a detailed analysis of relevant Community policies
or specific proposals for their reform.

The report is largely the result of intensive discussions within
a team of members of the Forward Studies Unit headed by
Christoph Bail and composed of Carlos Camino, Kees van Rij,
Michael Roberts and David Wright. Members of the team have
individually and collectively discussed the subjects of this report
with colleagues within the Commission as well as members of
research institutes within the Community and independent
experts. Three members of the team spent a week in

1

Washington and New York talking to a variety of experts within international institutions (World Bank, IMF, United Nations) and research institutes. Members of the team went individually to Geneva and Paris to discuss issues of the report with staff members of Unctad, GATT, OECD, the OECD Development Centre and independent experts. A draft of the report, finalized in December 1992, was circulated within the Commission and revised in the light of comments received. The report remains, however, a document established under the sole responsibility of the Forward Studies Unit. It engages neither the European Commission nor its services.

Summary

The report entitled 'The future of North-South relations –
towards sustainable economic and social development' contains
five chapters. Starting with reflections on the changed
geopolitical situation it goes on to analyse the evolution of
North-South relations and the development prospects, interdependencies and risks. On this basis, a global strategy for the
promotion of sustainable economic and social development is
proposed which in turn provides the background for suggestions for strategic priorities of the Community and its Member
States.

I. GEOPOLITICAL OUTLOOK: THE CHANGING NATURE OF NORTH-SOUTH RELATIONS

North-South relations are at a turning point after the end of the
East-West conflict. A new multipolar system is emerging at the
same time as the South as such is disappearing as a political
entity. Certain values such as democratic government, the rule
of law and a free market economy are becoming more
universally acceptable facilitating new forms of cooperation.
However, the concept of a 'new world order' remains unclear.
While the post-cold-war era offers greater opportunities for the
promotion of stability and security globally, local and regional
conflicts, contradictions and tensions are also gaining ground.
To deal with the latter and address more effectively the long-
term global challenges requires a strengthening of multilateral
approaches.

The European Community, in particular, has a strong

interest in promoting better global management of interdependence through a strengthening of multilateralism. It is at a crossroads between continued introspection and mounting external challenges requiring stronger international engagement and cooperation. It will, in particular, have to shoulder greater burdens in confronting regional instability in its eastern and southern proximity. However, in spite of its economic strength, the Community remains politically weak and will have to face resistance from Member States following divergent bilateral policies for which the possibilities have increased. This situation – and the necessity for the Community, in view of its geographical vulnerability, to ensure adequate burden-sharing notably with the other members of the triad – increases its interest in supporting multilateral approaches to overcome structural problems in North-South relations.

II. THE EXPERIENCE OF NORTH-SOUTH RELATIONS: LESSONS FROM THE PAST

This chapter attempts to draw the principal lessons of the experience (summarized in Annex 1) of North-South relations since the Second World War. A review of the evolution of development thinking suggests that there has been a somewhat circular evolution of theories and strategies moving in and out of fashion, but also a considerable learning process towards the integration of political, economic, social and environmental dimensions of development into comprehensive concepts. There is now a sense of crisis which, however, concerns not so much development thinking as the capacity of political systems to translate concepts into action.

It has become evident that the determining factors which have led to a widely divergent evolution of the economies of developing countries must be sought primarily in the way that the domestic policies of these countries have adjusted to local conditions and responded to their situation in the global economy and the geopolitical arena. Judging from past experience, developing countries need to assume more responsibility for their own development and adopt strategies guided by three principles: their policies must be centred on people, satisfying their needs and enlarging the range of their choices; they should adopt coherent economic policies promoting macroeconomic stability and improving the competitive environment for business; they should concentrate on better governance in terms of accountable political institutions, efficient administrations and budgets reflecting consistent long-term development priorities.

Development cooperation remains a positive and necessary concept. However, it generally does not seem to have had a decisive influence on the evolution of developing countries. Moreover, there is a sense of failure as far as the efficiency of traditional development aid is concerned. This has become evident by the shift to structural adjustment policies which, however, were also open to criticism in terms of their short-term focus on correcting external and budgetary imbalances, their negligence of sustained growth and their negative social and environmental side-effects. Past experience would favour an intensified policy dialogue with developing countries, more effective donor coordination and concentration of economic assistance on countries demonstrating a will and a capacity to pursue credible economic, social and environmental policies. Concessional aid should be concentrated on the poorest countries and targeted to people-centred development improving, in particular, education, training, sanitary conditions, family planning, food security and the preservation of natural resources.

The evolution of developing countries has been strongly influenced by the political strategies of the two superpowers and their allies to gain and maintain influence. Moreover, in the context of an increasingly globalized economy which developed

5

spontaneously in a climate of growing deregulation, the trade and macroeconomic policies of industrialized countries and the Organization of Petroleum Exporting Countries (OPEC) had decisive effects on the evolution of developing countries. The so-called North-South dialogue, due to an atmosphere of ideological confrontation, has produced few meaningful results. The multilateral trading system, because of its many loopholes, has done too little to ensure that developing countries benefit from their comparative advantages and the international division of labour. Policies addressing the problems of the deteriorating terms of trade for developing countries have not sufficiently taken into account the characteristics of the goods and markets concerned. The monetary and financial systems, due to systemic shortcomings, have not ensured an adequate flow of capital and investment to developing countries. Their failures relate, in particular, to the international allocation of savings, the emergence of negative financial transfers from the South to the North, the inadequate mechanisms to coordinate macroeconomic policies and to regulate financial markets and an insufficient stimulation of productive investments.

III. DEVELOPMENT PROSPECTS, INTERDEPENDENCIES AND RISKS: LESSONS FROM THE FUTURE

This chapter attempts to draw some lessons from an evaluation of long-term development prospects, interdependencies and risks. It looks, in particular, at how the deep underlying trends in population growth, poverty and environmental degradation are likely to interrelate and influence the future of both the North and the South. An extrapolation of present trends reveals that the chances of a major part of the world's population 'catching up' is becoming more remote unless there is fundamental change. The combined effect of poverty and population growth will intensify such global challenges as the spread of disease, the drug trade and, in particular, refugees and migration. Global environmental threats will increase as the result of a combination of rising poverty and overconsumption; atmospheric and water pollution are expected to increase, the degradation of the marine environment and of the soil to continue, tropical forests to disappear and biodiversity to be substantially reduced.

These deep trends can to some extent be influenced through a reorientation of economic, social and environmental policies. The economic outlook for the different regions of the world is extremely diverse. It is particularly bleak for sub-Saharan Africa. In turn, economic forecasts are influenced by a number of factors such as access to capital and markets, demand pull from industrial countries, adjustment to globalization, peace dividends and political stability. The chapter closes with two scenarios, one highlighting the risks for the North and the South as a consequence of an extrapolation of a 'business as usual' trend, the other highlighting possible gains for all as a consequence of gradual change to sustainable economic and social development.

IV. A GLOBAL STRATEGY FOR THE PROMOTION OF SUSTAINABLE ECONOMIC AND SOCIAL DEVELOPMENT

The global strategy proposed in the fourth chapter attempts to respond to the changed geopolitical situation and face up to the future challenges of interdependence in the light of past experience. It is based on:

(a) the concept of good governance of the southern, northern and eastern countries which must accept their responsibilities for the internal, external and 'boomerang' effects of their policies;

7

(b) the concept of global governance to deal more adequately with the opportunities unleashed by economic globalization and the increase in global risks; and

(c) the concept of sustainable economic and social development combining the ideas underlying such notions as human development, sustained economic growth and environmental sustainability in a multidimensional approach.

The strategic orientations suggested consist firstly in the promotion of deep economic integration in the context of the establishment of a multilateral trade organization and a more comprehensive regulatory multilateral framework for trade and investment beyond the General Agreement on Tariffs and Trade (GATT), including the establishment of objective criteria for market access, emphasis on regulatory convergence in the interest of combining the reduction of distortions of competition with the necessity to achieve public policy objectives, multilateral rules on investment and competition including, in the long term, the establishment of an international competition agency and coordinated actions to correct structural problems in certain commodity markets. In the short term, measures are necessary to ensure a more stable flow of financial resources to developing countries, including alleviation of debt servicing repayments and reduction of debt stock overhang for heavily indebted low-income countries as well as an improvement of prudential, fiscal and accounting rules. In the longer term, the establishment of new regulatory mechanisms to influence international liquidity and a strengthening of the International Monetary Fund (IMF) are envisaged. The World Bank system, including regional development banks, should be provided with additional resources to channel more effectively concessional aid and to act as an intermediary between the international financial markets and developing countries in order to guarantee the latter financing on favourable and stable terms.

Secondly, certain measures to stimulate sustainable economic growth are suggested, namely:

(a) better coordination of the macroeconomic policies of industrialized countries;
(b) incentives in favour of new environmentally friendly growth sectors;
(c) support for strengthening South/South, South/East and East/East economic links through regional integration schemes, financing of triangular trade transactions, the establishment of a clearing system covering trade within and between these regions, the facilitation of triangular technological cooperation and the promotion of inter-regional networking;
(d) a reinsurance scheme covering foreign investments against certain political and legal risks and a multilateral facility to overcome prohibitive costs for small and medium-sized companies to identify investment opportunities.

Thirdly, a new range of policies is necessary to implement Agenda 21, adopted at the 1992 United Nations Conference on Environment and Development (UNCED) in Rio. A number of suggestions are made to help reorient development towards environmental sustainability through increasing knowledge of the ecological costs and benefits of different development patterns and policies on the basis of 'green' accounts, appropriate pricing to reflect external costs, ecological tax reforms and transfers of resources and technological know-how to developing countries.

Fourthly, the central concept of establishing long-term development contracts between major donors and recipient countries is outlined. These policy frameworks, building on the experience under the Lomé Convention and within the Bretton Woods institutions, would contain commitments for both sides as suggested in Chapter II and aim at securing coordinated financial and technical support for policies ranging from family planning, development of human resources and capacity-building to the stabilization of the macroeconomic foundation, structural adjustment, rural development and the protection of natural resources.

To facilitate global governance, suggestions are made to transform gradually the international institutions in order to strengthen global policy initiation, legitimization and implementation. To ensure global policy coherence, it is proposed to clarify the tasks of the various institutions and to strengthen the mechanisms of coordination and global policy orientation. This would preferably lead to a revitalization of the role of the United Nations (UN) and its specialized agencies in the economic and social areas, implying either a redefinition of the mandate, composition and functioning of the Security Council or the establishment of a UN sustainable development council. Finally, it is suggested to promote and strengthen regional cooperation and integration in order to conciliate the necessity for better management of interdependencies with the specific needs and features of proximity reflecting the diversity of cultural values and models of society.

V. A STRATEGY FOR THE EUROPEAN COMMUNITY AND ITS MEMBER STATES

The last chapter looks at the priorities of the Community and its Member States in contributing to the global strategy outlined in Chapter IV. The Community, which by its own nature tends to define policies reflecting a diversity of interests and which possesses some of the key elements of 'soft power', should be in the best position to promote such a strategy. A definition of the Community's geopolitical priorities on the basis of risk avoidance and an efficient internal division of competences and tasks leads to an emphasis on systemic issues related to the management of global interdependencies and on regional responsibilities in terms of managing its geographical proximity.

On this basis, it is suggested that the Community concentrates on policy areas where it clearly has an added value in comparison with individual Member States and not simply act as a 13th donor. It should become a full participant in the multilateral organizations that regulate trade, finance and monetary relations and exercise leadership in defining global priorities in such areas as peace and security, democracy, protection of human rights, demography, poverty, environment, migration, pandemics and drugs, as well as initiate and coordinate common actions. It should concentrate its efforts on the initiation and coordination of systemic policies to overcome structural shortcomings and increase its budgetary means for common actions in support of such policies. In return, it could leave the implementation of its development cooperation policies largely to Member States and, where appropriate, specialized domestic and multilateral agencies. This would imply a progressive shift from geographically defined cooperation policies to horizontal and systemic policies and multilateral approaches. The Community should assume a leading role in promoting a coherent multilateral strategy based on 'development contracts'. Such a multilateral approach should, in particular, concentrate and increase efforts to overcome the structural problems faced by sub-Saharan Africa whose development prospects are bleakest. It would imply a fundamental reorientation of the Lomé scheme.

The Community's second main geopolitical interest is to promote peace, stability and development in its direct neighbourhood. It should therefore upgrade its policies towards the countries in Central, Eastern and South-Eastern Europe and the Mediterranean region, including the countries of the former Soviet Union, Turkey and the Middle East. *Vis-à-vis* the Central and East European countries, this would mean 'deep' integration on the basis of a progressive implementation of the

11

four freedoms leading eventually to full membership. *Vis-à-vis* the non–Community southern Mediterranean countries, this would mean the creation of an economic cooperation zone progressively leading to a free trade area with the Community. Economic integration within each region through free trade areas (FTAs) customs' unions or cooperation agreements should be encouraged as steps towards integration into the economy of the Community. In terms of assistance policies, existing financial protocols should be gradually replaced by structural funds.

The Community would also have to ensure greater internal policy coherence with respect to the objectives of sustainable economic and social development. This concerns primarily agricultural and trade policies to eliminate progressively trade restrictions and distortions affecting developing countries, and also industrial, R&D, fiscal, energy and environmental policies as well as the generation of additional resources for the financing of sustainable development strategies (e.g. through energy taxes).

Finally, a number of suggestions are made to involve European citizens and increase public awareness of global interdependencies and risks because, in the final analysis, nothing less than a profound reorientation of the production and consumption habits and social values underlying Western society is required. These suggestions include a greater political role for non-government organizations (NGOs); planning for the adoption and implementation of long-term strategies when risk awareness in the public is high; the formation of a voluntary Community service of qualified young citizens of all Member States serving together in developing countries; a code of conduct for EC companies; the floating of a Community-wide solidarity loan and twinning between EC and southern cities. The shift towards new patterns of consumption and production will be greatly aided if new technological choices and economic analysis tools become available. The development of such tools would require action to direct basic and applied technological research towards the advancement of environmentally friendly products, the reduction of energy consumption, appropriate technologies suitable to be transferred and diffused in developing countries and instruments to measure the real social and environmental costs of economic activities.

Chapter I

Geopolitical outlook: the changing nature of North-South relations

1. NORTH-SOUTH RELATIONS AT A TURNING POINT

The world that is emerging after the sea changes of recent years is very different from the world as it has developed after the Second World War and the process of decolonization. The East-West conflict and North-South dualism no longer provide an adequate framework in which to understand global political trends. The defeat of communism obliges countries to reposition themselves in the light of increasing transnational interdependence, both in terms of benefiting from the opportunities offered and of containing the risks involved. It heightens their awareness of deep destabilizing trends such as population growth, rising poverty and the depletion of natural resources interacting with political disorder and economic mismanagement, to produce international chaos. The possible further destruction of the tropical forest, the danger of malfunctioning nuclear power stations in Eastern Europe, the threats of the use of atomic, biological and chemical (ABC) weapons in the Middle East, and the possibility of a *coup d'état* in Moscow are all perceived as having similar planetary significance. Under the dynamism of economic globalization, a new division of labour is replacing traditional East-West and North-South divisions. Consequently, the division of the world along political lines is being replaced by a categorization of countries and regions in accordance with their stages of development. Moreover, existing structures and practices in international relations rooted in the concept of sovereignty of nation States and favouring bilateralisms are no longer adapted to the realities of interdependence, globalization and regionalization. Against this background, this chapter describes the main geopolitical trends and vulnerabilities resulting from increasing interdependencies and argues that a strengthened multilateralism corresponds to the Community's interest in promoting stability in international relations.

1.1. The emergence of a multipolar system

The collapse of communist rule in Central and Eastern Europe and the former Soviet Union has led to the abrupt termination of the cold war in Europe and other parts of the world. The traditional bipolar world, mainly characterized by security considerations and military power, has ended. The world is increasingly characterized by multipolarity, a situation in which different poles are exercising different kinds of power in safeguarding their interests, cooperating in order to prevent or temper conflicts and managing the increasing economic, social, technological and environmental interdependencies. From a military/security point of view, the United States of America remains the only superpower. From an economic/financial perspective, the EC (with a strong emphasis on Germany), the USA and Japan constitute the main poles of a multipolar system that had already strongly developed before the end of the East-West conflict. Russia, although threatened by continuing internal disintegration, will remain for the time being an important military pole and Third World countries such as

China and India remain formidable demographic poles with considerable military and economic potential. But within this multipolar conglomerate, the balance of power is dramatically changing, not only because of the disappearance of the Soviet Union, but also because of the relatively diminished economic power and indebtedness of the USA to the benefit of Japan, the newly industrialized Asian countries and China, and a more integrated and enlarged European Community. The significance of this evolution towards multipolarity is increased by a broadening of the concept of security to include new risks of a non-military nature. The emerging new poles are, however, not simply a continuation of the old poles. The complexity of the distribution of power and the role of public opinion make it increasingly difficult for governments to impose unilaterally policies on their own people and on other countries. Therefore, multipolarity will be less hegemonic and less hierarchical, and leadership will increasingly be based on the exercise of soft power, by stimulating and convincing other actors to go in a certain direction.

It has been argued[1] that the emerging system of international relations is apolar rather than multipolar, leading to an absence of order rather than a limited degree of disorder. However, whatever the qualifications attributed to the post-cold-war international system, in essence it will be, more than in the bipolar era, dependent on the interactions between the different poles in managing their interdependences and avoiding potential conflicts. On the other hand, it seems highly improbable that the world will move towards unipolar stability, based on the exclusive primacy of the USA, as has been suggested by commentators[2] and a recent Pentagon study. Indeed, one of the main trends in the new global arena is that no single country is any longer able to exercise power and influence everywhere. Increasingly, international coalitions of cooperating nations seek to assume specific collective responsibilities, such as in the Gulf War, the former Yugoslavia and Somalia.

1.2. The disappearance of the South as a political entity

While the former Eastern bloc countries attempt to find their place as close as possible to the West, and some Asian countries of the former Soviet Union seek closer cooperation with Turkey or Iran, in the South the disappearance of Soviet communism has reinforced the trend to growing heterogeneity. The South as a separate category hardly exists any more and the term 'Third World' seems to be justifiable only in the sense that, like the *tiers état* in pre-1789 France, it is a highly diverse class that is chiefly characterized by being excluded from the political decision-making process. Developing countries are increasingly divided between newly industrializing countries (the four Asian tigers, some countries of ASEAN but also countries like Mexico and Turkey) that are in a process of transition to 'northern' status, and underdeveloped countries fighting against decades of economic stagnation, uncontrolled demographic growth and an increasingly marginal status in the world economy.[3] Several former Eastern bloc countries (in particular the Asian republics of the former Soviet Union, but also Albania, and, arguably, Romania) find their place increasingly in the South, and show characteristics of underdevelopment such as economic backwardness and severe poverty. This trend could lead to what J.-C. Rufin[4] calls 'un nouveau grand schisme' between North and South in which the North integrates certain economically promising southern countries, creates a 'limes' between North and South composed of a number of buffer States, and leaves the rest of the South cut off and isolated (mainly sub-Saharan Africa). However, the territorial and political boundaries of such a limes are difficult to define and also cut right through countries. Moreover, this schism resulting from the exclusion of entire regions from the global economy is at least partially checked by the vital interests of the North in solving such long-term problems as saving forests, reducing greenhouse gas emissions, managing transnational migration, enforcing (nuclear) non-proliferation, fighting terrorism, drugs and pandemics such as AIDS. These global problems give the developing countries growing leverage over rich countries because of their nuisance value.

1.3. The rise of democracy and free market economies

There is a global movement towards the introduction of democratic government, the rule of law and free market economy, not only in the former communist regions of Europe and Eurasia, but also in Latin America, Asia, Africa and South Africa. The acceptance of the market economy by most countries in the Third World is one of today's major ideological shifts, and coincides with the emergence of new elites that have buried traditional anti-Western attitudes. By radically reforming economic and financial policies, a country like Mexico, which was considered a difficult case a few years ago, has reversed negative trends by curbing the inefficiencies of strong government interventionism and protectionism. Similar developments are visible in, for instance, India, Vietnam, China, Brazil and Argentina.

Apart from factors such as increased opposition against inefficient, repressive dictatorships (South Korea, Philippines), lost wars (Argentina/Falklands) and economic pressures (isolation of South Africa), the most important impetus to change towards more democratic rule has been the globalization and intensification of communication (which includes the increased role of the press, non-governmental organizations and private pressure groups) and the effects of international economic exchanges which cannot be stopped at borders and leads people to demand more representational government structures and freedom oriented policies. The Western culture of consumerism has long attracted southern and eastern citizens and pulled them away from repressive governments and planned economic systems. Although the global trend towards democracy is far from consolidated and from being irreversible, its breakthrough is also closely related to the breakdown of the power systems in Eastern Europe and the former Soviet Union and the disappearance of the ideological opposition between Western and communist alternatives for development and justice, notably in the Third World.

Although democracy is gaining ground, it should be emphasized that it is not a uniform Western-style democratic model that is applied in most countries. The Confucian-flavoured democracies in North-East Asia demonstrate that democracy can be combined with collectivistic traditions and a certain degree of authoritarianism. In other words, democracy is generally strongly influenced by specific local traditions and challenges. In countries where democracy rule has been introduced, the rule of law, respect for minorities and human rights are still far from being respected. There also seems to be a growing consensus among the international community that there is a kind of collective 'right of interference' in situations where acute humanitarian crises occur and basic human rights are suppressed in a context of civil war, such as in the former Yugoslavia and Somalia.

1.4. Technological revolution and globalization of markets

The technological revolution and the globalization of markets are profoundly affecting international relations. Technological change, the communications revolution, the role of multi-national corporations and private-sector strategies transcend national borders and reduce the influence of the nation state as an international actor. This process is widening the gaps not only between the rich industrialized and the poor under-developed countries, but also within the developing world. Most southern countries are falling increasingly behind the North because they have less access to capital, technology and qualified personnel. This consequently increases inequalities between rich and poor, both between and within countries, cutting through national borders and creating a North in the South and a South in the North.[5] In the North, this social exclusion has evident dangers of increasing social tensions, particularly of an ethnic nature. Reactions against artificially imposed and mishandled Western-type modernization in some southern countries have led, and are likely to continue to lead, in several cases to a revival of anti-Western ideologies.

2. NEW FORMS OF COOPERATION AND TENSIONS

2.1. The phantom of a 'new world order'

Some commentators have suggested that several of the above-mentioned trends, some of which were already visible before the developments in Eastern Europe, are now formulated in the concept of a 'new world order'. This concept was launched by President Bush, during the Gulf crisis in September 1990, shortly after the fall of the Berlin Wall and was increasingly discussed in the North and South, as the Central and East European countries started their long and painful march towards the establishment of democracy and free market economies. The Gulf War, which occurred at a crucial point in time, was the first occasion for the international community in the post-cold-war era to deal with a major conflict. The result was that Saddam Hussein's aggression was condemned internationally (countries from the South included) and contained by force under US leadership under the aegis of a UN mandate. However, this war also opposed northern and southern countries in the sense that many countries and people in the South saw the conflict as a war between rich and poor, Christianity and Islam, modern Western technology and values and southern cultures. As such, the 'new world order' is as much a northern concept to define 'new ways of working with other nations towards peaceful settlements of disputes, solidarity against aggression, reduced and controlled weapons' arsenals and just treatment of all peoples' (President Bush), as it is seen by many countries in the South as a concept destined to serve Western self-interests.[6] In any event, it is clear that the concept President Bush had in mind is largely limited to security in a traditional sense, and does not extend to economic, social and environmental risks. The United Nations Conference on Environment and Development demonstrated the limitation of this US concept of world order.

This Conference in Rio was another culminating point in addressing global issues in the new international context in which North-South relations were severely tested. Although a number of agreements were signed and general commitments were made, the North, divided on important issues, failed to reassure the South about the even-handedness of its commitment to sustainable development, since financial aid remained limited and largely uncommitted and technological transfer a vague promise. Population growth was omitted from the agenda and the conference failed to adopt a credible strategy to fight poverty. The USA was almost entirely isolated, Japan failed to live up to the expectations of it as a new economic superpower and paymaster, and the EC was on several major issues unable to agree on a credible common line. Equally, the South was largely divided, the G77, due to its growing heterogeneity, having enormous difficulties in presenting common views.

2.2. The world between multipolarity and multilateralism

Thus, the emerging international geopolitical situation appears to distinguish itself mainly by its complex and untidy nature, thus defying attempts to characterize it through grand statements, neat categories and simple formulas. Indeed, the new world order is far from being the blueprint of a world in which democracy, free market and the rule of international law reign in an era of peace and stability.[7] The present situation should rather be characterized in terms of oscillation between multipolarity (including polarization between regions) and multilateralism in which actors seek to redefine their changing relationships against the background of these global trends and challenges. Both the Gulf crisis and the global security issues at stake at the Rio Conference demonstrate that the challenges of interdependence will have to be met through the continuing adaptation of traditional political structures to the increasingly transnational economic, social and environmental realities, i.e. by strengthening multilateralism. However, it must be emphasized that the majority of marginalized urban and rural poor in both southern and eastern, and even in northern countries, do not necessarily share the experience of a world in a transitional phase: to these people poverty and social exclusion seem permanent and continue to deteriorate.

2.3. Opportunities for stability

Obviously the post–cold-war era offers greater opportunities for the promotion of stability and global security because the end of the East-West conflict in all its political, military, economic and ideological aspects is bringing about an increased capacity to cooperate and jointly face common crises, define common interests, guarantee common security and shape a common future on the basis of a common responsibility.[8] The Gulf War has shown that it should be possible for the North and South to act jointly on the basis of a common set of principles including, in particular, renunciation of territorial expansion by violent means, giving democratic and economic development first priority, involvement of all countries with no country being isolated and the abandoning of ideological confrontation in favour of overall agreement on purpose. The main powers that largely dominate the so-called 'new world order' – the USA, the EC as a whole, Japan, Russia and, to a lesser extent, China – seem to agree, in varying degrees, on these basic principles. There are some signs that key countries in the South such as Brazil, Mexico, Argentina, Egypt, South Africa, Turkey, India, Indonesia and South Korea are evolving in the same direction.

Countries that use force on their neighbours or minorities within their borders (Iraq, the former Yugoslavia) and countries in which *coups d'états* are staged (Haiti, Peru) are increasingly and more effectively (not necessarily more efficiently) condemned by the international community. The UN Security Council has increased its capacity to deal with international crises and its security role is now generally accepted by UN members. Evidence of this is the recent initiatives to institutionalize and strengthen preventive diplomacy, peace-keeping and peace enforcement.[9]

The new international context, for example, has made it possible to get rid of the taboos surrounding arms sales to, and military expenditure by, Third World countries. There has been a tendency that, while Northern countries concluded arms reduction agreements (e.g. USA-Russia), many Third World countries continued to build up arsenals with the connivance of the North. International security arrangements, such as the UN weapons register, now seek to limit world trade in military equipment. Increasingly, the IMF, World Bank and other agencies and donors look at military expenses in relation to expenditure on education and health in Third World countries. The discussion on peace dividends is thus not limited to reducing military expenditure in rich countries, but also deals with the nature of public expenses in poor countries.

Although its success was limited, the Rio Conference has demonstrated that a global North-South dialogue is possible, overcoming the previous existence of two opposing blocs defending irreconcilable positions. But the Rio Summit is, as said above, far from being the herald of a new world order. Equally, the Uruguay Round has the potential to contribute to increasing global stability. A growing number of countries from the South and from the former communist world have joined and thus strengthen a process that seeks to liberalize economic and commercial relations between regions and countries on a global level.

2.4. Conflicts, contradictions and tensions

The post-cold-war era has also demonstrated that conflicts, contradictions and tensions in the North and South are gaining ground. The formerly perceived image of global security being entirely dependent on the balance between the USA and the former Soviet Union, is being replaced by a highly diffuse, fragmented picture of threats to global security.

First, there is a growing number of conflicts based on violent ideology, such as Islamic fundamentalism, and nationalism. Apart from 'established' conflicts (e.g. the Arab-Israeli conflict, North-South Korea, Cyprus, Kashmir) new conflicts have developed after the break-up of communist rule in Europe, involving the Asian republics of the former Soviet Union, Russia itself, Moldova, the former Yugoslavia, and possibly other East European countries. The explosion of nationalism and ethnic tension in Europe and the former Soviet Union is, of course, a direct consequence of the political vacuum that resulted from the disappearance of oppressive but unifying communist rule. These social tensions are, however, not limited to the eastern part of Europe. They also manifest themselves in several EC Member States, in particular in Germany, but also in France, Italy, the United Kingdom and others, where they are the expression of a more general malaise with the way the democratic system functions.

The idea that the end of the cold war has necessarily brought a universally accepted normative orthodoxy based on liberal democracy is challenged, not only because of strong differences between cultures on how democracy is exercised, but also because of the continued existence of powerful countervailing forces based on violent ideology in several Third World countries, such as fundamentalism in the Middle East, strong subversive movements like Sendero Luminoso in Peru and the Tamil Tigers in Sri Lanka.

Many smaller countries in the Third World are able to buy or build modern weapon systems (even nuclear weapons) and are no longer under the influence of one of the superpowers who used to play a moderating role in regional conflicts. The availability of huge stocks of arms (including ABC weapons) threatens international stability, especially in the Middle East and the Maghreb. Although the USA is still the main Western actor in this area, Europe and Japan will have to increase their contribution to conflict prevention.

Second, growing international interdependence also has a tendency to provoke conflicts as a consequence of population growth, poverty and migration movements, and the growing gap between North and South with regard to economic performance and social conditions. Conflicts are unlikely to occur between the North and the South as such, but rather between individual industrialized and developing countries or among developing countries. Apart from the well-known disputes concerning access to non-renewable resources such as oil, problems of food security and access to water could lead to serious regional conflicts. Growing population and migration pressures are likely to lead to quarrels over immigration and the closed-door policies of richer countries. For example, as the European Community consolidates its emerging common immigration policy, tensions with the Maghreb and Eastern Europe could very well increase. Furthermore, conflicts over the environment and public health issues such as AIDS and drugs could easily lead to conflicts between northern and southern countries.

3. THE STRENGTHENING OF MULTILATERALISM

The transitional phase in which the post-cold-war world finds itself is thus characterized by the disappearance of the clear-cut East-West division and overriding political antagonism between North and South. The contradictions and tensions are sharpening between, on the one hand, the tendencies towards the globalization of democratic values and free market economies and, on the other hand, the fragmentation generated by nationalism, ethnocentricity and violent ideologies. This situation is in constant flux and the main actors are in the process of repositioning themselves with regard to what they perceive to be the opportunities to build a new global security system, while safeguarding their specific interests. This requires renewed efforts to meet the long-term challenges of sustainable economic and social development and the medium- and short-term threats to an increasingly interdependent, and therefore highly vulnerable, system of international relations.

The degree to which these existing highly interdependent global economic, social and environmental interrelations can be effectively controlled and steered will depend upon the existence and acceptance of adequate political structures. The combination of traditional bilateralism between nation States and limited multilateral arrangements in some specific areas no longer provides a stable framework in which the world's main challenges can be resolved. The long-term solutions regarding the structural North-South integration can only be realized through the adaptation of obsolescent political structures to the realities of interdependence, globalization and regionalization of economic, social and environmental forces. This implies a much strengthened multilateralism, and a fundamental reform of the United Nations.

4. THE EUROPEAN COMMUNITY IN A NEW INTERNATIONAL CONTEXT

4.1. The Community at a double crossroads: between introspection and international engagement

During the cold war, the Community mainly concentrated on its internal development, consistent with its political origins in the 1950s aiming towards building peace among the Member States through economic integration. Early on, the Community developed external policies, but these were largely limited to trade and development cooperation linked to the colonial heritage of its Member States. In the era of the East-West division, stability in Europe was assured through the existence of the nuclear protection shield of the USA and NATO's defence policy. Since the early 1970s, intergovernmental European political cooperation has progressively become an important mechanism in developing common positions on international affairs, however essentially only in a limited, reactive manner, and generally not replacing the bilateral foreign policies of Member States. The Community has gradually become an economic world power, but has kept a low profile in the political and security areas. The profound changes of recent years are driving the Community towards assuming a more active role in international affairs, as confirmed by the Maastricht Treaty, whilst at the same time risking renewed inner divisions among Member States on the direction and means of foreign policy. As a result, it is likely to remain heavily oriented towards its internal and wider regional problems. The two main external challenges that the Community faces in the years ahead are likely to be the promotion and implementation of policies that stabilize and support the processes of transformation in Central and Eastern Europe, northern Africa and the Middle East, and the assurance that its vital interests in the global political and economic context are not eroded.

28

To meet both these challenges, the Community has a strong interest in preventing, in the longer term, the Third World becoming more fragmented and marginalized from the industrial North. Failure to integrate progressively the southern economies into the international economy is likely to increase tensions and systemic political instability, both in the Community's proximity as well as further away, generally affecting the northern welfare States. It is to be expected that the Community, more than the USA or Japan, is the actor in the best position to take the lead in strengthening multilateral cooperation, which is due to its historical links to the South, and the unique nature of the Community model based on cooperation between States.

4.2. Confronting regional instability

The dynamic rebirth of the Community in the second part of the 1980s occurred in a still divided continent. The single market goal of 1993, the implementation of the Single European Act, the goal of economic and monetary union (EMU), in short internal integration and deepening of the Community, were driven essentially by economic considerations.

However, the Community entered a drastically different context after the fall of the Berlin Wall. Europe has since evolved from a relatively stable and safe place, guaranteed by the threat of mutually assured destruction, into an increasingly unstable and highly turbulent continent, confronted with a revival of nationalism, ethnic minority problems, civil war, fragmentation and dismemberment of existing States (Yugoslavia, Czechoslovakia), the creation of new States (former Soviet Union successor States), aggressive fundamentalism and threats of mass migration from Eastern Europe and northern Africa, acute environmental threats, including malfunctioning nuclear power stations, proliferation of weapons and even isolated

29

famine. Problems that had been buried for decades in Europes past and were mainly associated with today's Third World are becoming facts of life in Europe again, and have brought the problems of North-South integration much closer to home.

As East European States, EFTA members, Mediterranean and north African countries seek to join or strengthen their relationships with the Community, and the traditional political and security frameworks find themselves in a process of transformation or have disappeared, the Community is driven by the maelstrom of regional political changes and events in Eastern Europe, and northern Africa, to play an active role in reducing the various risks pertaining to adjacent sources of instability.

However, the Community's means to conduct a more coherent common foreign and security policy remain limited. The provisions of the Maastricht Treaty are largely based on intergovernmentalism, which, generally speaking, only allows reaction to events rather than the formulation of *ex ante* common policies.[10] The difficulties in formulating and implementing strong common policies in Eastern Europe are demonstrated daily (e.g. the former Yugoslavia) and it will take the Community considerable time to grow into its new role of environment-maker in the larger European region.

The necessity for stronger common policies in post-cold-war Europe also runs the risk of being eroded by a creeping tendency towards divergence and tension between the Community's main Member States on fundamental objectives. The sudden absence of a common enemy has, paradoxically, widened the possibilities for formulating bilateral policies. Even Germany and France have demonstrated important differences over such policy priorities as NATO versus the WEU (Western European Union), Eastern Europe versus northern Africa, and enlargement. A more assertive Germany in foreign and security affairs will not necessarily follow its privileged partner, France, on issues it considers to be of vital importance. France and the UK, both permanent members of the UN Security Council, are likely to continue to conduct strong bilaterally oriented foreign policies. Italy and Spain are drawn into more active foreign policy in the Balkans, the Mediterranean, and Latin America. The Netherlands, Denmark, Belgium, Portugal, Greece, Ireland and Luxembourg all seek, to varying degrees, to keep a sufficiently large room for manoeuvre in foreign and security policy. This is not to say that these tendencies will prevail over trends towards deeper foreign policy integration, in view of the fact that the Community is seen by most Member States as a necessary platform for a more effective promotion of their foreign policies.

Moreover, even if these tendencies towards fragmentation and introspection in the Community, described by Cohen-Tanugi as an unidentified political object,[11] continue to frustrate more coherent and assertive common policies towards Central and Eastern Europe and northern Africa, the pressure on the Community to promote actively stability in its wider region will remain strong.

In any event, there is a danger that the Community will, probably for a considerable period of time, remain insufficiently equipped to engage in external bilateral policies the way its Member States, or, for that matter, Japan and the USA, do. It is therefore probable that its comparative advantage will, for the time being, remain primarily in the multilateral economic-commercial area. As a result of its internal structure and experience in building on and overcoming the diversity of cultures and national interests, it may also have a comparative advantage in the context of interregional dialogue and cooperation.

4.3. Promoting better global management of interdependence

With the end of the cold war, the importance of political and ideological dividing lines in the world has generally declined while that of economic and social dividing lines has grown. Since the Community is the largest and most open trading bloc in the world, and since it does not dispose of the necessary strong bilateral policy tools that nation States traditionally use in the pursuit of their interests, it has a strong interest in promoting further (deep) integration between the triad economies while at the same time strengthening the multilateral dimension in order to facilitate the progressive integration of the Third World into the global economy. But the balance in the coming years is not necessarily in favour of multilateralism, even though there is increasing economic interdependence between the main trading blocs.

Economic interdependence contains a considerable potential for conflict and tension among industrial countries. Growing tensions between the USA, the EC and Japan on economic issues could lead to rising protectionism, managed trade or even the emergence of antagonistic trade blocs, of which the main victims would be in the Third World. As long as the communist world served as a common enemy, common political and security considerations tended to be stronger than disagreement on economic issues. Now that the common security threat is largely removed, political relations between the three are increasingly focusing on problems related to their economic interdependence. The different strategies followed by them in the quest for market shares and technological advantages could become conflictual in case of persistent strong imbalances. Relations between the USA and Japan, for example, are already leading to political tensions, which could, in the longer term, affect the politico-military alliance between the two countries, in the sense that Japan could be tempted to promote a more assertive and independent foreign policy, especially towards Asia. In order to contain the threat of antagonistic trade blocs, the Community should use its experience and potential economic leverage to strengthen multilateral disciplines and institutions.

The institutional framework and the mechanisms of economic regulations devised by the North are neither adapted to the new forms of global economic interdependence, nor to the need to integrate southern countries in the international economy. Consequently, global economic interdependence leads to the increasing marginalization, if not exclusion of, many Third World countries from the benefits of the globalization of (financial and commercial) markets and threatens in the long term the viability of North-South economic relations and, therefore, global economic security. To facilitate their integration, the Community should promote substantial reforms in the management of global interdependence assuring, in particular, adequate representation of the divergent interests.

A strengthening of the multilateral dimension is also necessary to ensure adequate sharing of the financial, commercial and political burdens which the North needs to shoulder *vis-à-vis* the South. The regions surrounding the Community are arguably both politically less stable and economically less dynamic than the regions bordering on the USA and Japan. If Europe were left alone to ensure stability in its region, this could affect its own well-being and its international competitiveness to a disproportionate extent.

On the other hand, multilateralism is a better guarantee of an adequate presence of the politically weak Community in economically dynamic regions outside her geographical proximity, such as South-East Asia, as compared with exclusive reliance on bilateral strength.

Notes

1 Laïdi, Zaki (ed.), *L'ordre mondial relâché*, Paris, 1992.
2 See Krauthammer, C. 'The unipolar moment', in Allison, Graham and Treverton, Gregory T. (eds.), *Rethinking American security: Beyond cold war to new world order*, New York, Norton, 1992.

3   Kahler, M., 'The international political economy', *Foreign Affairs*, autumn, 1990.
4   Rufin, J.-C., *L'empire et les nouveaux barbares*, Paris, 1991.
5   Emmerij, Louis. *La grenade dégoupillée*, Paris, 1992.
6   In fact, many Third World intellectuals and some politicians accuse the West of measuring with double standards: the 'Western' decision to bomb Iraq ('Islamic') cities was much easier to take, than a decision to reciprocate likewise by the 'West' against Serbian ('Western') aggression in ('Western') Bosnia-Herzegovina. The decision of the United Nations, stimulated by Secretary-General Boutros Ghali, to act decisively and swiftly in Somalia somewhat corrects this perception.
7   Freedman, L. 'Order and disorder in the new world', *Foreign Affairs* No 1, 1992.
8   L. Emmerij, at the conference 'Scanning the future', The Hague, 1992.
9   'Preventive diplomacy, peacemaking and peacekeeping', report of the Secretary-General of the United Nations, June 1992.
10 Within the intergovernmental structure of NATO coherent politico-military doctrine was only possible because of the specific security conditions of the cold war and the particular (nuclear) role of the USA.
11 Cohen-Tanugi, L., *L'Europe en danger*, Paris, 1992.

Chapter II

The experience of North-South relations: lessons from the past

This chapter builds on the experience of North-South relations summarized in Annex 1. It attempts to identify shortcomings and positive messages resulting from the evolution of development thinking, domestic policies of developing countries, development cooperation and the operation of the international economic system dominated by the North. It seems important to try to understand this experience in order to get a grasp on the future.

1. DEVELOPMENT THINKING: A PAINFUL LEARNING PROCESS

Looking back at the evolution of development thinking, one is struck by the manner in which theories and strategies have moved in and out of fashion in a seemingly circular movement and by the current absence of innovatory approaches. Modernization theories focusing on rapid industrialization and growth imitating Western models were popular in the 1960s, put aside in the 1970s and re-emerged in the 1980s under the cover of structural adjustment. Reformist responses focusing on employment, redistribution with growth and basic needs were

35

promoted in the 1970s, fell victim to the debt crisis and Reaganomics in the 1980s and reappear now in reports concentrating on strategies centred on people. Structuralist theories which had explained underdevelopment by exogenous factors and promoted autonomous strategies such as ISI (import substitution industrialization) as well as radical global reforms such as the NIEO (new international economic order) seem to have lost their appeal in the face of the successes of the newly industrialized countries (NICs) and the collapse of communism. However, the environment/development debate has revealed that structuralist approaches in favour of radical departures from the liberal-capitalist paradigm still have some appeal.

On the other hand, there has also been a considerable learning process and a *rapprochement* of basic positions. Neoliberals today tend to accept the existence of social and environmental costs in industrialization and structural adjustment processes and recognize an important role for the State and for multilateral cooperation to correct market failures. Reformists today tend to recognize the importance of functioning markets and trade liberalization for development.

Most analysts now recognize that the causes of underdevelopment are neither just home-made nor exclusively attributable to the international system, but must be found in a combination of endogenous and exogenous elements. Abstract blueprints are out of fashion as it has become evident that development strategies must be multidimensional and adjusted to the particular situation of a country. All this has at least facilitated a dialogue beyond ideological boundaries based on the analysis of socioeconomic realities and country-specific interests. It has led to what may be called a new orthodoxy of development thinking integrating the economic, social, environmental and good governance dimensions into comprehensive concepts, such as sustainable human development.

There is nevertheless a perception of crisis in development thinking or at least among development thinkers which can only be explained in part by the fact that the long-standing bitter controversies between modernizers, reformers and structuralists have come of age. It relates to the experience that reality has kept neither the promise of rapid growth through industrialization, except in very few cases, nor the hope that basic needs can easily be satisfied through redistribution strategies nor indeed the aspiration for autonomous development through self-reliance. As analysts increasingly recognize that the world is characterized by the seemingly immutable and mutually reinforcing trends of economic globalization, social marginalization and environmental degradation, many share a feeling of impotence. Many seem to have come to the conclusion that solving the problem of underdevelopment is primarily a matter of governmental and non-governmental actors assuming responsibility with respect to the formulation and implementation of coherent strategies at the different levels. If so, the perceived crisis is not so much one of development thinking but of translating concepts into action, i.e. of the way in which political systems work.

2. DOMESTIC POLICIES OF DEVELOPING COUNTRIES: THE IMPORTANCE OF STRATEGIC CHOICES

The determining factors which have led to the widely divergent evolution of the economies of developing countries must be sought in the fashion that the domestic policies of developing countries have been adjusted to local conditions and tailored to respond to their situation in the global economy and the geopolitical arena. In the past, governments of developing countries have tended to seek the causes of their poor performance in unfavourable external conditions. Today, the catchwords of self-reliance favoured by the South and good governance favoured by the North contain the same message, namely that developing countries must assume more responsibility for their own development.

Searching for a uniform development strategy for all regions of the world is futile. Abstract blueprints, however refined, have never worked. Strategies must build on the cultural heritage and dynamic forces of individual societies. Similarly, it is dangerous to focus exclusively on one segment of society or on one policy area. Simplistic recipes for progress only breed new distortions and rigidities. However, past experience teaches us that development strategies should be guided by three principles. They should be centred on people, satisfying their basic needs and enlarging the range of their choices. They should adopt coherent economic policies promoting macro-economic stability and improving the competitive environment for business through market-friendly policies. They should concentrate on good governance through accountable political institutions, efficient administrations and budgets reflecting consistent development policy priorities.

2.1. Investment in human resources

Experience, in particular in Asia, tells us that the reduction of poverty, the management of demographic transition and long-term development strategies require in the first instance adequate and effective investment in human resources. Limited budgetary means should therefore be targeted towards primary education, basic health care and the provision of safe water. They should also be targeted to effective population policies calling, in particular, for an expansion of female education, the reduction of infant mortality rates and an extension of family planning services.

People-centred development further requires strategies to increase the economic participation rate of the poorest segments of the population.[1] This has implications first of all for rural development policies in terms of promoting small-scale labour-intensive agricultural activities and better access to land ownership, credit and domestic markets. The priority given in many developing countries to industrial and urban development and large-scale export-oriented agriculture has impoverished rural areas and led to massive migrations to the cities, which have only a limited capacity to absorb labour in formal employment. The spread of urban slums and an informal sector of labour-intensive activities caught in a vicious circle of low productivity, low income and low investment in turn calls for the improvement of access to basic services, credit for small-scale business and legal protection. The informal sector accounts for some 50% of all economic activity in Latin America alone and, according to some researchers, is growing into an increasingly important engine for economic growth, especially where economic overregulation stifles entrepreneurial enterprise at the micro-level.[2]

2.2. Coherent economic policies

In economic terms, governments which have been most successful have stabilized the macroeconomic foundation of their economies, keeping, in particular, fiscal deficits manageable and inflation under control, and have adopted market-friendly approaches, improving the climate for business and diversifying their economic base.[3] In some of the most successful countries transformation processes have been supported by targeted industrial and trade policies on the basis of strategic political choices. However, in general, governments should refrain from intervening in areas where markets work and promote competition as the most effective means of stimulating an efficient use of resources, innovation and investment. Governments need to concentrate their activities on those areas where markets alone cannot be relied upon: the provision of basic services, education and training, adequate infrastructures, the promotion of indigenous research and the protection of the natural environment.

Agricultural policies

In all, 60% of the developing world's population rely on agriculture for their living.[1] However, the agricultural sector has fallen victim either to neglect or deliberate discrimination in the development strategies of developing countries which have often contained an industrial and urban bias. Where governments introduced agricultural policies, it was usually in support of monoculturalists producing export crops which yielded, in the short term, higher export income, but made farmers and governments dependent on unstable world prices and led to the displacement of food crops onto more marginal land. It has been estimated that the negative effects of developing countries' policies pursued in other sectors of the economy or at the macro-level represented on average a 27% tax on agriculture.[2]

The resulting loss of competitiveness and decline of the agricultural sector, in the context of high population growth, resulted in urban migration and so further increased urban population pressures. Low-cost food thus became a political priority at a time when the North was becoming an area of structural overproduction and swamping the world markets with subsidized exports. As competition between the agricultural powers (not just in the North) intensified, the real price of imported food for developing countries decreased, undercutting domestic production.

In the longer term, the effect of importing this subsidized food has been to alter consumer tastes causing a shift in the pattern of demand away from traditional basic staples towards other cereals, and especially towards animal products. The net result has been a rising import dependence which, when combined with low levels of income and entitlements, has led to food security problems which are likely to become more acute in the future, despite sufficient production to feed the world population. Developing countries' dependence on food imports is likely to increase, with the Organization for Economic Cooperation and Development (OECD) estimating that the import bill will increase by 143% for North Africa and the Middle East, 293% in Latin America and 350% for sub-Saharan Africa.[3]

The net result for the peasant farmers of the developing world has been one of decline. Reductions in fallow periods leading to declining soil fertility and erosion occur as farmers try to safeguard their domestic food supplies and produce more food for the market to increase their incomes. Hence a vicious circle develops in which population pressure makes traditional production techniques environmentally and economically unsustainable. Given the challenge of providing adequate employment for the growing active population in the developing world, the continued neglect of agriculture will cause considerable economic dislocation and continued environmental degradation. In sum, without a revitalization of the agricultural sector in developing countries, their economies will stagger under the burden of feeding and employing their growing number of people.

Notes

1 The number is projected to fall to just over 50% by 2000 and regional differences are strong. For example, in Latin America the agricultural sector employed under 30% of the population as compared with over 70% in Africa in 1985. Alexandratos, N. '1988 world agriculture: Towards 2000', An FAO study.
2 Brown, Martin and Goldin, Ian. 'The future of agriculture: Developing country implications', OECD Development Centre, 1992, p. 115.
3 *Ibidem* p. 97.

In order to benefit from globalization, countries should open progressively domestic economies to international trade and investment. This is not to say that free trade is or has been the magical solution to development problems. The experience of the newly industrialized economies has shown that a certain level of protection of the agricultural sector may be necessary to keep rural populations on the soil and guarantee a reasonable level of self-sufficiency (see box). Also, a carefully adjusted degree of protection in favour of infant industries during a limited period may be necessary to manage the transitional phase of industrialization. However, the failure of badly managed import substitution policies has shown that protracted protectionism leads to exclusion from technological progress and economic marginalization. Participation in economic and technological progress requires participation in international competition. The intermediate step of regional integration, which could have served to strengthen the domestic economic base in order to be better equipped for global competition and at the same time reduced the dependence on North-South trade, has not been seriously tried by developing countries in the past but would seem to offer good potential, in particular if built around growth poles.

It also needs to be stressed that specific strategies which have worked in one context cannot simply be transposed into another. The success of the 'Asian tigers' took place against a particular historical, regional and sociocultural background. The local conditions and the external environment that allowed these countries economies to take off are not easily reproduced. For example, Latin American countries with a long tradition of workers' rights would find it difficult to adopt, without serious social upheaval and a weakening of democratic institutions, the working practices and social conditions that were the lot of the new Asian economies. They therefore have greater difficulty becoming internationally competitive in the manufacture of products requiring a high intensity of unskilled labour. In products with greater value-added requiring more skilled labour, access to the requisite technology requires the development of professional skills and institutional capacities through strong educational, technological and sectoral policies that most of these countries lack.[4] As a result of economic adjustment policies, some developing countries will embark on the first stage of export-led growth, but very few will be able to move on to the second stage without large-scale reforms affecting the structure of the State and society as a whole.

2.3. Good governance

With respect to the governance dimension, we may distinguish between constitutional, administrative and budgetary aspects. Human development obviously requires respect for universally recognized basic human rights and fundamental liberties (in particular, those of expression, association and movement) as well as equality before the law. However, past experience does not provide a conclusive answer to the question of the relationship between democratic government and economic development. It can neither be generally maintained that democracy is a necessary precondition for economic development nor that it is an obstacle to it. In Asia, most regimes steering the industrialization process were authoritarian. In Africa, authoritarian leadership tended to resist necessary change and breed corruption. Latin America suffered from military dictatorships, corrupt elites and populist regimes. The current transition problems in Eastern Europe and the Commonwealth of Independent States (CIS) also show that the parallel processes of democratization and economic liberalization are not necessarily mutually supportive. Western models of democracy cannot simply be exported at all stages and imposed on different cultural and social settings. Strong central leadership may be necessary for the management of difficult adjustment and transition processes, but socioeconomic development also requires increasing levels of political participation and involvement of all groups of society in the decision-making process. Such participation requires essentially:

(a) access to information concerning decisions to be taken;
(b) transparency and reliability in the decision-making process;
(c) opportunity for all groups of a society to express their views and influence the decision-making process;
(d) the ability to hold the decision-maker accountable.

In sum, political (as well as economic) participation is in principle supportive of development. However, imposing Western-style political pluralism, irrespective of the cultural traditions and historical evolution of particular societies, is potentially counterproductive.

There is a more obvious positive correlation between economic development and 'good governance' in the narrower sense of adequate government institutions, legal frameworks and administrative capacities.[5] The role of governments in providing public goods, establishing rules to make markets work effectively and correcting market failures tends to be even more important in developing countries than in developed countries. The symptoms of poor governance are excessive regulation, misallocation of resources and arbitrariness in the application of laws. Reforms of public-sector management tend to be complex and slow, involving both the parastatal sector (often calling for large-scale privatization) and the civil service (often lacking transparency, predictability and accountability). Technical assistance in this area can produce lasting positive effects provided cultural differences are adequately respected.

Finally, a number of recent major studies have provided a clearer understanding of the correlation between financial resource management and economic development. In particular, the United Nations Development Programme (UNDP) *Human development report 1991*, contains a detailed analysis of the public spending of developing countries and relates this to an index merging income with life expectancy and literacy to serve as a measurement for human development. It finds that nearly USD 50 billion a year – about 2% of the GNP of the developing countries – could be released for more productive purposes. This could come mostly from freezing or reducing military expenditure absorbing 5% of the GNP of the developing world, halting capital flight, combating corruption, reforming public enterprises and reducing internal policing. Moreover, the UNDP report gives detailed evidence of the correlation between social expenditure towards human priority concerns (basic education, primary health care, safe drinking water, family planning and nutrition programmes) and progress in human development suggesting the need for considerable reallocations of expenditure in many countries.[6]

3. DEVELOPMENT COOPERATION: A SENSE OF FAILURE AND A SHIFT IN CONDITIONALITY

3.1. Efficiency of traditional development aid

In the face of 40 years of development cooperation, many commentators express a sense of failure. Most continue to support its necessity even if they criticize that development aid has not been sufficiently targeted to the reduction of poverty.[7] Indeed, development cooperation extending beyond aid remains a crucial concept and assistance has had beneficial effects in many cases. However, cooperation and assistance do not seem to have had a dominating influence on the economic and social evolution of most developing countries, not even those which managed to leapfrog into industrialization. Bilateral assistance can even be said to have had detrimental effects to the extent that it was designed to meet the short-term or strategic political, security or economic interests of donor countries, that it was not adapted to the socioeconomic and cultural conditions in the recipient countries and that it stabilized inefficient, if not corrupt, political structures. Moreover, the lack of coordination among donors often pursuing conflicting goals has hampered the elaboration and implementation of coherent development strategies by recipient countries.

There is, in particular, a growing scepticism about the efficiency of traditional forms of project aid channelled through the governments of recipient countries. This lack of efficiency is, on the one hand, due to the duality and rigidity of economic, social, administrative and political structures in recipient countries, which often lack the capacity to absorb the aid received and ensure that it translates into a lasting amelioration of their capacity to develop. The trickle-down effect of investments through programmes and projects has generally only occurred in environments where the basic conditions necessary for an economy to flourish were assured through coherent macro-economic, sectoral and social policies. In countries lacking the political will and administrative capacity to elaborate and implement sound development strategies, the impact of outside assistance tends to be lost and unfortunate side-effects in terms of dislocation, wastage and creaming-off may occur.

Inefficiencies of development aid are, on the other hand, due to a lack of responsible behaviour on the part of donors. In particular, bilateral assistance is still given largely in the form of tied aid, which according to recent studies reduces its efficiency by more than 15% of the aid provided.[8] An insufficient proportion of aid is targeted to social priority areas, while for some countries it has essentially been an instrument of foreign policy and mainly taken the form of military aid. While the aid provided by multilateral institutions tends to be more targeted to the poorest countries, it has not always been sufficiently adapted to local needs. The administration of project assistance by donors often still lacks a proper selection and follow-through process. Also, developed countries all too often take away with one hand what they have given with the other, as can be demonstrated by examples of market access restrictions affecting the export of products from factories and farms financed by the country imposing the restrictions. Moreover, as long as the East-West conflict endured, donor countries saw little interest in challenging elites in countries belonging to their respective spheres of influence, irrespective of the extent of their corruption.

Within the wide network of Community cooperation policies, the Lomé system stands out not merely because historically it is the most extensive cooperative relationship ever established between developed and developing countries, but also because of its innovative approach based upon a collective and multidimensional policy dialogue and a pioneering mechanism for the stabilization of export revenues. However, due to a lack of flexibility, the system has not always provided enough incentives for positive efforts by Lomé countries and may in certain cases have helped to perpetuate incoherent economic policies and stabilize corrupt political leaderships. The hesitation of applying political and economic conditionalities to relationships with countries having only recently acquired independence was understandable and contrasted positively with the political interference strategies of the rivalling superpowers. However, it had to be recognized that unconditional assistance did not help developing countries to become fully accountable for their policies, allowed economic dependence to continue under the guise of a convenient safety net and caused many countries to become addicted to aid. As a result, much more emphasis is put not only on economic and technical, but also on political conditions under present Community policies.

The importance of non-governmental organizations (NGOs) in development cooperation has strongly increased during the last decades, both in terms of intensity and finance. NGOs are often particularly effective because they more easily adapt to the local, social and cultural conditions that are necessary to implement projects successfully, and because their projects are often small, concrete, precise, and limited in time. However, NGOs can only be successful if they operate in a general framework of sound macro- and mesoeconomic policy, which remains the responsibility of governments. Outside such a framework, NGOs run the risk of creating no more than limited islands of temporary relief. A sound understanding of the distribution of tasks between NGOs and governments, each respecting each other's autonomy – which often is not the case – is therefore essential. Too much reliance on NGOs can have two other negative effects: undermining the national and regional policies of central administrations, which are already relatively weak in many southern countries, and reinforcing the brain drain from the government to the private sector, in which the NGOs occupy an important place.

In general, experience has shown that developing countries who make credible efforts to apply good governance and sound economic policies may benefit from external support for investments which would not otherwise take place and have better access to the international capital market. In countries lacking both good governance and sound economic policies, externally financed investments are unlikely to lead to lasting economic development. In these countries, assistance must concentrate on the satisfaction of basic needs and relief.

3.2.   Structural adjustment

Under the guidance of the Bretton Woods institutions, priority has been given to the allocation of available resources to programmes of recipient countries designed to reform their economic policies. The shift in focus to structural adjustment, technical assistance programmes for training in public- and private-sector management and institution-building points in this direction.

However, in drawing up structural adjustment programmes,

the multilateral institutions have tended to focus more on correcting external and budgetary balances than on growth (postponed to the second stage of structural adjustment) and the special circumstances of the countries concerned.

The theoretical models on which these programmes were based initially were static taking no account of the effects of budgetary and monetary variables on the level of activity and on the informal sector, or of developments in the international economic environment that call for a capacity for adjustment and responses from economic and political operators and that in no way correspond to the real situation of the poorest developing countries.[9]

Structural adjustment programmes have been particularly successful (in terms of balance of payments and export growth) in countries with adequate levels of human capital, physical and social infrastructure and performing institutions (mostly in Asia and some Latin America countries), while they have generally failed in countries facing serious structural problems (in particular, Africa).

Moreover, in a considerable number of cases, structural adjustment programmes of the past decade have had serious negative social and environmental effects and have led to sharp drops in investment, jeopardizing future growth. However, the IMF and, in particular, the World Bank are becoming more sensitive to such criticism and we now see the emergence of a new generation of structural adjustment programmes that draw on the lessons of past failures.

In any case, adjustment lending should be linked to changes in the international environment and the special circumstances of the countries concerned. As demonstrated by the role played by the Interamerican Development Bank since 1985, a greater role for regional organizations and institutions in the framing of such programmes is helpful from this point of view and also to encourage more coordination between adjusting countries in the same region.

On the same lines, the timetable for the adoption of measures should be better tailored to the situation of the country in question and, in particular, trade liberalization and price liberalization implemented gradually so that supply can adjust and producers gear up to face competition. In the final analysis, adjustment cannot be the result of a narrowly defined blueprint, but only of a comprehensive reform process which takes time and depends on the capacity of a country to design and implement reforms with the fullest participation of the members of its society.

3.3. Key points

In sum, past experience would favour an intensified policy dialogue with developing countries focusing on the conditions of good governance, more effective donor coordination and concentration of economic assistance on countries demonstrating a will and capacity to pursue credible economic, social and environmental policies. Concessional aid should be concentrated on the poorest countries and targeted to people-centred development: education, training, sanitary conditions, food security, family planning and the preservation of the environment. The procedures for implementing aid should be tailored to a participatory development model with an emphasis on decentralization and involvement of the people concerned.

4. THE INTERNATIONAL ECONOMIC SYSTEM IN THE QUEST FOR REGULATORY COHERENCE

The external factors that have most influenced the evolution of the developing countries are the political strategies employed by the two superpowers and their allies to gain and maintain influence and the trade and macroeconomic policies of the industrialized countries and OPEC coupled with the functioning of an increasingly globalized economy.

This globalization of the world economy, which gained momentum in the 1970s and 1980s, developed spontaneously in a climate of growing deregulation. Its main effects were of little benefit to most developing countries. In its third report on human development, the UNDP estimates that dysfunctions in the structure of global markets (including labour mobility) are causing the developing countries to lose about USD 500 billion a year, i.e. 10 times the amount of development aid that the industrialized countries grant them each year.[10]

The so-called North-South dialogue has produced few tangible results because it was largely conducted on the basis of ideological North-South confrontations, countries being locked into rigid group structures (such as the Group of 77 representing developing countries except China, and Group B, representing OECD countries) which did not reflect the diversity of substantive interests. In this confrontational atmosphere, it was extremely difficult to bridge gaps, build up majorities of moderates from both sides and come to reasonable and meaningful conclusions.

4.1. The international trade system

(a) GATT and the Uruguay Round

The multilateral trading system has been relatively successful in bringing down tariffs and other trade restrictions and preventing trade wars. In the 1980s, the value of merchandise trade grew by 4.8% per year. However, developing countries' exports grew by only 1.6% and their share in world trade, which had risen from 17.9% in 1970 to 28% in 1980, fell back to 21% in 1990, due in part to the evolution of the oil price.[11] Moreover, the major portion of trade expansion of developing countries remained with very few countries. Generally speaking, there

51

have been too many loopholes in the multilateral trading system to allow developing countries to benefit fully from comparative advantages and the international division of labour, even though some countries (i.e. the NICs) managed to profit from the system as a consequence of carefully planned policies favouring export-led growth.

GATT disciplines applied essentially only among Western industrialized countries. Under the shield of special and differential treatment and exemptions for balance-of-payments restrictions, most developing countries remained largely outside international competition. In recent years, many of them have, however, opened their economies unilaterally in the framework of structural adjustment policies. On the other hand, the GATT did not prevent developed countries from heavily protecting their economies against exports from developing countries. Agriculture and textiles remained essentially excluded from GATT disciplines allowing protectionist and distortive market interventions to the disadvantage of developing countries. In other areas, new forms of non-tariff trade barriers (such as voluntary export restraints), tariff escalation and anti-dumping measures prevented developing countries from benefiting from comparative advantages. It has been estimated that developing countries suffer annual losses of USD 75 billion from trade restrictions.[12]

The Uruguay Round negotiations have attempted to address these shortcomings, extend multilateral disciplines to new areas (such as the protection of intellectual property rights and the liberalization of trade in services) of importance not only to industrialized countries but also for the integration of developing countries into the world economy and tighten the legal and institutional regime. However, even a positive outcome of the Round will leave foreign trade regimes widely disparate because market access remains largely the result of bilaterally negotiated concessions rather than objective criteria. These disparities can produce serious economic and ecological imbalances.[13] Moreover, the absence of binding international competition rules leaves markets which are outside the jurisdiction of northern competition authorities largely unprotected against international cartels or abuses of companies having a dominant position of market power.

Developing countries are generally expected to gain from a strengthened and extended multilateral trading system. Universally applicable and enforceable rules counterbalancing protectionist forces, unilateral discriminatory actions and bilateral deals tend to work to the advantage of smaller countries and weaker economies otherwise exposed to the law of the jungle. Asian and Latin American countries are likely to reap important benefits from trade liberalization, while poor African countries may suffer in the short term from the erosion of their preferential margins.[14]

The Uruguay Round process also saw for the first time a more active involvement of many developing countries in trade negotiations and the formation of subject-specific coalitions of interest across traditional North-South dividing lines, such as the Cairns Group of non-subsidizing exporters of agricultural products.

(b) Terms of trade of developing countries

In the last decade, most developing countries saw their terms of trade worsen considerably. If 100 is taken as an index of the terms of trade of the developing world in 1979, this index had fallen below 70 by 1990. This trend may be ascribed mainly to declining commodity prices (including oil) and most developing countries' failure to diversify their export base; it is as much a consequence of local factors as of the industrialized countries' commercial policies towards the developing world.

The evolution of the relative prices of exports and imports largely depends on the characteristics of the goods concerned (e.g. elastic/inelastic, inferior/superior, etc.). For products for which demand is relatively inelastic (tropical products and most raw materials), and for which world demand is constantly shrinking in the face of substitutes, systems for stabilizing export earnings and preferences granted by the industrialized countries to certain developing countries have had conflicting results. While these instruments have attenuated the budgetary and balance-of-payments tensions caused by worsening terms of trade, they have also done much to encourage an over-production that entrenches the erosion of world prices for the products concerned.

Faced by the pressing need to obtain foreign exchange rapidly (first to cover imports and investments and then to repay the debt), the countries on the receiving end of these instruments have neglected export diversification and concentrated instead on increasing their production capacity, ignoring the fact that their competitors were doing the same and overlooking the inelasticity of demand for these products.[15] The inevitable consequences of this behaviour have been falling prices, the paralysis of export diversification efforts, a worsening of the terms of trade of the developing countries concerned, a contraction in their export earnings, the failure of the systems for stabilizing export earnings, and an increase in the debt problem. The financial resources currently devoted to the stabilization of export earnings might arguably be better employed as direct support for the balances of payments of the countries concerned and for projects aimed at diversifying their export base.

The impossibility of implementing and financing buffer stocks and the conflicting interests of the different producers have led to the failure and abandonment of most multilateral commodity agreements aimed at stabilizing prices by controlling supply.

In the case of products for which demand is more elastic,[16] the main reasons for the failure of the systems of preferences granted by the industrialized world must be sought in the reduced margins of such preferences and in the commercial and fiscal policies implemented by certain developing countries.

For instance, in many developing countries (and this is particularly true in the ACP (African, Caribbean and Pacific States), export taxes are a major source of budget revenue, neutralizing the preferences granted, reducing the competitiveness of national producers and discouraging investment. Several countries which benefit from free access to the Community market for most or all of their industrial products refuse to accept that trade concessions should be granted to other developing countries, fearing the erosion of a margin of preference they scarcely use.

In sum, past experience suggests that diversification and export promotion are of greater long-term benefit than the granting of preferential margins which are, in any event, progressively eroded.

4.2. Monetary and financial systems

During the 1980s, the international flow of credit and investment towards the developing countries was negatively affected by their worsening economic and political situation (implying a growing political and financial risk particularly for commercial creditor banks and for private multinational corporations), as well as by the eruption of the debt crisis (particularly as regards Latin America and sub-Saharan African countries). As a consequence, investment lending became more prudential, selective and concentrated in those developing countries (such as some fast-growing economies in South-East Asia) showing more promising growth prospects and offering more interesting profit opportunities. These interconnected phenomena accelerated the progressive marginalization of many heavily indebted low- and middle-income countries which not only were cut off from the international capital market but experienced declining foreign direct investment as well as considerable capital flight. Further analysis suggests, however, that the marginalization of many developing countries in the international movement of capital also results from the operation of the machinery for the international allocation of world savings and, ultimately, the monetary and financial system.

(a) International allocation of world savings

The dearth of funds for financing economic growth in developing countries can in theory be attributed to a lack of international savings or to a dysfunction in the way in which such savings are internationally allocated. Although the propensity to save has diminished in recent years in several industrialized countries, it would be difficult to ascribe the current rationing of productive investment essentially to a shortage of international savings. In 1992, world savings amounted to 21.5% of GDP, which is roughly equal to previous periods (except for an average of 25% during the 1976–80 period), and reflects a sharp reduction in the USA, a slight decline in the EC and a considerable increase in Japan.[17] However, this body of savings is no longer invested in the same way.

The globalization of the international financial system in the last two decades was first reflected in a greater integration of the industrialized countries' financial markets and of these financial markets and 'off-shore' financial centres. For this reason, and in view of the fact that most developing countries do not have international banks capable of growing in this new environment, the globalization of the financial system has most benefited the industrialized countries and in particular their public and financial sectors. The increasing mobility of capital has in particular allowed a large part of international savings to be steered towards financing the budget deficits of certain industrialized countries.

The disparities between, and the lack of effective coordination of, the industrialized countries' macroeconomic, financial and monetary policies are contributing, through rising real interest rates and volatile exchange rates, to an increase in economic uncertainty and shortages of resources at reasonable rates for developing countries.

Furthermore, the current functioning of the international financial markets leads to paradoxical situations that hinder investment in the productive sector and jeopardize economic growth, both in industrial and developing countries. For example, short-term interest rates have been for a number of years and still are higher than long-term ones and no-risk short-term investments are more profitable than long-term risks. Therefore, the international capital markets operate at present on a short-term basis that sometimes favours speculation and often discourages productive investment. This situation calls for more effective regulation of the financial and monetary markets (through appropriate prudential rules), reduction of fiscal deficits in major industrial countries and closer international macroeconomic coordination. In view of the globalization of markets and in order to prevent free-riding, such measures should be set at world level and cover all markets.

(b) Financial transfers and debt

Over the last few years, there has been a radical shift in the pattern of external financial flows to developing countries from debt to equity financing and from bank to non-bank sources.[18] Within this overall pattern, there is a growing gap between developing countries that can have access to the private capital markets for bank loans, bonds and stocks and those that cannot. Those countries which avoided debt restructuring or which have successfully reduced their commercial bank debt in the context of the Brady plan provisions and in the framework of a comprehensive structural adjustment effort have been able to regain capital market access, attract new foreign direct investment (FDI) and encourage the repatriation of flight capital. By contrast, severely indebted low- and low-middle-income countries with largely official debt (as is the case of most of sub-Saharan African developing countries) still have little realistic prospects of access to long-term private lending for the foreseeable future. Moreover, the official bilateral and multi-lateral flows in the 1970s and 1980s to the poorest countries remained insufficient to cope with the growing financial requirements of these countries and to offset the consequences of procyclical lending, leading to important net financial transfers on long-term lending from the South to the North.[19]

In this respect, it is worth mentioning that the economic situation of a number of developing countries (which are dependent for most of their export earnings on raw materials) has seriously deteriorated due to the fluctuation in the world market prices for these products. In times of strong world economic growth, prices for raw materials have generally risen and public spending and imports by developing countries have tended to grow at a rate equal to or greater than export earnings. The return of harder times and lower prices for basic products are then reflected in very substantial budget deficits and foreign debt. At the same time, the lenders have based their decisions on current solvency and failed to give due weight to long-term trends or the bankability or quality of projects.

Conversely, in hard times, when loans are most needed to restore growth and solvency, the donors (fearing insolvency or even default) apply much stricter bankability criteria. In other words, the international financial operators apply non-dynamic risk criteria and do not always manage to distinguish between the risks of illiquidity, insolvency or default.

Cancelling the debt could in these conditions have perverse side-effects: it would not re-establish the creditworthiness of the countries concerned and in the long term make possible a new debt cycle. A lasting solution to the debt problem therefore would have to go to the root of the phenomenon of procyclical lending.

(c) The role of the international financial institutions

The IMF and the World Bank are no longer acting as regulators of the debt cycle, their loans in the 1980s having already matured. They contributed to the financial outflow from developing countries to the tune of nearly USD 8 billion per annum during the period 1987 to 1989 in the case of the IMF and USD 500 million in 1991 in the case of the World Bank.[20] The debt cycle that results from the procyclical behaviour of the private commercial banks and national public lenders is aggravated by the lack of additional resources stemming from those institutions, given the financial constraints to which they are themselves subject. The World Bank which, according to its terms of reference, was intended to act as an intermediary between the international financial markets and the developing countries so as to secure for them financing on favourable terms, only partially fulfils this role since it is itself subject to the ups and downs of a disorderly world financial market. The IMF, whose original function was to guarantee the stability of the International Monetary System and to limit fluctuations in the financial cycles, lacks resources and powers to monitor and control international liquidity.

The lack of mechanisms to regulate the international financial markets tends to render the debt phenomenon procyclical, a feature that cannot be mitigated by the IMF and the World Bank. Lacking the resources that would enable them to operate such regulatory machinery, these institutions have focused their efforts on stabilization and structural adjustment programmes which have helped to stabilize the international financial system, but partly at the expense of the developing countries' long-term prospects.

(d) Direct investment

Many experts, and in particular those of the IMF and World Bank, rightly emphasize the crucial role that foreign direct investment could play in the restoration of a positive balance in North-South financial transfers. It should, however, be noted that in the period 1980–90 most direct investment flowed into the industrialized countries. If an index of 100 is ascribed to the average annual flow of direct investment in the five-year period 1975–79, this index had by 1989 reached 767 for the industrialized countries compared with only 356 for the developing world.[21]

In 1991, FDI made a positive contribution to the developing countries of roughly USD 7 billion (in net terms: new investment less repatriated profits).[22] The bulk of these positive transfers, – which follow many years in which profit repatriation exceeded new investment (a USD 2.4 billion deficit in 1970, a 5.2 billion deficit in 1980 and a USD 0.2 billion deficit in 1985) – concerns only the most dynamic South-East Asian countries and, to a lesser extent, some of the highly indebted countries of Latin America.

In the case of the newly industrialized countries of South-East Asia, such investment has, in fact, created new production capacity. By contrast, in Latin America it has largely taken the place of existing debt (debt for equity swaps) or has been used to acquire existing firms without creating new production capacity and without involving any actual transfer of foreign exchange. The remaining developing countries continue to receive no or very little foreign direct investment.

Moreover, in several developing countries, many opportunities to make investments of which the strictly economic return would in theory be guaranteed are neglected owing to the political risk which discourages foreign investors.

In any event, and even in the case of those countries that are currently in receipt of a positive flow of foreign investment, profit repatriation is likely to increase more rapidly than new investment. The Overseas Development Council[23] takes the view that in the year 2000 repatriation of profits from the developing countries could amount to USD 50 billion (as compared with USD 17.4 billion in 1991), while new investment would amount to roughly USD 55 billion (as compared with USD 24.5 billion in 1991). A net balance of approximately USD 5 million would, quite clearly, not be enough to offset the negative transfers stemming from commercial debt and the other mechanisms referred to earlier.

Foreign direct investment brings other more important benefits that cannot be assessed in terms of the balance of payments, namely transfers of technology and increased exports. An analysis of the effects of foreign investment on the balance of payments, however, especially when the phenomenon of profit repatriation is taken into account, shows that foreign direct investment is not in itself enough to guarantee the financial transfers needed by the developing countries, and, in particular, those which are heavily in debt.

5. THE NEED FOR REFORM

In sum, the increased poverty and marginalization of many developing countries are the result of inadequate policies in these countries, detrimental policies of developed countries and costly failures of the international system. Efforts towards more efficient development cooperation policies on the basis of increased conditionalities and policy dialogues should not serve as a pretext for ignoring the necessity for the adjustment of other policies of industrialized countries, such as agricultural, trade, financial, monetary and energy policies which may have destabilizing effects on developing countries. A better performing North-South dialogue would need to cover all areas of interdependence which determine the global environment and result both in more effective support for long-term domestic development strategies and correction of systemic failures in the international system. Such a global dialogue would seem to require a considerable reform and strengthening of the international institutions ensuring both a better representation of the interests of developing countries and more coherence in global management.

Notes

1 See, in particular, Dutch Government report, 'A world of difference – A new framework for development cooperation in the 1990s', The Hague, 1991, pp. 159 et seq.
2 de Soto, Hernando. *El otro sendero*, Lima, 1986.
3 For a comprehensive analysis of the paths towards economic development see, in particular, the World Bank World development report, 1991, 'The challenge of development'.
4 See Bustelo Gómez, Pablo. 'Economía política de los nuevos países industriales asiáticos', *Siglo Veintiuno de España*, Madrid, 1990.
5 For a detailed analysis of these questions, see the World Bank paper 'Managing development: The governance dimension', 1991.
6 According to the UNDP report, a sounder basis for the reallocation of social expenditure could be established through monitoring of the public expenditure ratio (public expenditure as part of national income), the social allocation ratio (percentage of public expenditure earmarked for social services), the social priority ratio (percentage of social expenditure earmarked for social priority concerns) and the human expenditure ratio (percentage of national income earmarked for human priority concerns). The report concludes that the human expenditure ratio needs to be at least 5% if a country wishes to do well on human development.
7 See, in particular, R. Cassen & Associates, *Does aid work?*, 1986.
8 See World Bank, 'Global economic prospects and developing countries', 1993, p. 7.
9 The usual model is of the Mundell-Fleming type, which is

essentially a monetary approach to the balance of payments backed up with a Polack-type of absorption approach. What these approaches have in common is that they point the finger at monetary financing of the budget deficit as the principal cause of the external imbalance and leave out of the picture the role of the international environment (openness of markets, trends in the terms of trade, world growth, interest rates, etc.).

10　See the UNDP 'Human development report, 1992' p. 6.

11　GATT, *International trade 1989–90*; Unctad, Trade and development report, 1991; World Bank World development report, 1991.

12　Human development report, 1992, p. 6.

13　A case in point is the combined effect of low Community tariff bindings for manioc (6%) and soya meal (zero) and high duties on feed grains and cereals; see von Verschuer, H. *The future world economic order*, 1991.

14　For a detailed study, see Golding, J. and van der Meersbrugge, D. 'Trade liberalization: What's at stake?', OECD Development Centre policy brief, 1992. The authors estimate income gain from a 30% trade liberalization of between +2.6% for ASEAN and −0.2% for sub-Saharan Africa, p. 25.

15　The income elasticity and price elasticity of most raw materials and tropical products are generally low, which means that a reduction in the price of these products or an increase in the consumers' earnings leads to a relatively small increase in demand that cannot compensate the producers for the loss of earnings resulting from the fall in prices.

16　That is products for which a fall in prices or an increase in consumers' incomes is reflected by a more than commensurate increase in demand and therefore by an increase in producers' earnings, for example most industrial products and some top-of-the-range agricultural products.

17　See IMF, 'World economic outlook', May 1993, p. 193; and also World Bank World development report, 1991, 'The challenge of development', 1991, p. 23, Table 1.2.

18　World Bank; 'Global economic prospects and the developing countries', 1993, p. 1.

19　The 1983–90 average of these transfers was USD 21.5 billion annually; UNDP Human development report, 1992, p. 50. However, aggregate net transfers (net flows, less interest payments and profit remittances) have been positive since 1989 both overall and for most regions except Latin America; World Bank, *ibidem*, pp. 4–5.

20 *Source*: UNDP Human development report, 1992, pp. 5 and 51.
21 *Source*: Turner, P. 'Capital flows in the 1980s: A survey of major trends', *BIS Economic Papers*, No 30, Basle, 1991.
22 A modest amount that is more or less equivalent to the cost to the developing countries of a 1% increase in international interest rates.
23 Overseas Development Council, 'Debt reductions and North-South resource transfers to the year 2000', Policy Essay No 3, Washington DC, February 1992.

Chapter III

Development prospects, interdependencies and risks: lessons from the future

Whereas the last chapter aimed to draw lessons from past experiences, this chapter aims to trace the principal factors which will shape future North-South relations. It begins by looking at how the deeper underlying trends in population growth, poverty and environmental degradation will interrelate and influence the future of both the North and South.[1] These deep trends will in turn be affected by the prospects for economic growth in developing countries and the wider world economy which are also outlined in the chapter. Finally, the chapter closes by elaborating two scenarios for the future, business as usual and a move to sustainable economic and social development, which, drawing on the lessons of the first three chapters, present a series of stark choices.

1. DEEP TRENDS IN POPULATION GROWTH AND POVERTY

1.1. Population growth

The post-war period has been a population watershed but the most optimistic scenarios of demographers still suggest a rise in world population from its current level of 5.3 billion to around 8 billion by 2015 and possibly to 12.5 billion by the middle of the next century.[2] A combination of factors – economic growth, improvements in living standards and stringent population policies – have brought reductions in the overall rate of population growth. However, the young age structure of these populations means that population growth has a substantial in-built momentum.

As the graph below illustrates, the highest population growth rates are to be found in the poorest regions of the world where 1.2 billion people are barely surviving in absolute poverty.[3] These population growth rates place pressure on the already strained economic infrastructure of developing countries and stretches the capacity of these economies to generate employment (particularly in the rural areas), so exacerbating existing social and environmental problems. *De facto*, these population growth rates require economic growth to at least match the rate of growth of population which in some cases means growth rates greater than 3%. High rates of population growth increase the propensity of migration both within countries (from rural areas to urban slums) and across frontiers – an important consideration for Europes southern flank.

Population growth needs to be understood in its social, religious and cultural context. Policies aiming at breaking the vicious circle of population growth, poverty and environmental degradation must be framed in this context. In general, increasing the income of poor households, reducing child mortality rates still further, expanding education and employment activities (especially for women) and improving access to family planning seem to reduce the rate of population growth.[4] Expanding economic opportunity is another crucial variable. It is therefore abundantly clear that population growth and poverty are inextricably linked and must be tackled concomitantly.

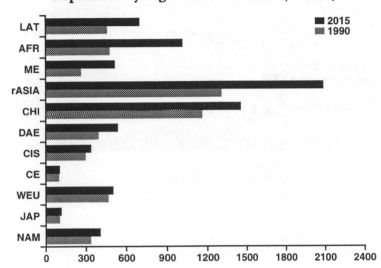

Population by region 1990 and 2015 (million)

Abbreviations: LAT: Latin America: South America, Central America and the Caribbean; AFR: Sub-Saharan Africa; ME: North Africa, Arabian peninsula, Iran, Iraq, Jordan, Lebanon and Syria, not including Israel; CHI: China; DAE: Dynamic Asian economies: Hong Kong, Singapore, Taiwan, South Korea, Malaysia, Philippines, Indonesia and Thailand; CIS: Commonwealth of Independent States; CE: Central Europe: Poland, the former Czechoslovakia, Hungary, Bulgaria and Albania; WEU: Western, northern and southern Europe, including the former Yugoslavia, Israel and Turkey, but not Albania; JAP: Japan; NAM: North America: USA, Canada, also including Australia, New Zealand and South Africa; rASIA: Rest of Asia, including Melanesia, Micronesia and Polynesia.

Sources: The medium variant projections. United Nations, 'World population prospects 1988', New York, 1988; 'Scanning the future. A long-term study of the world economy' 1992, pp. 240 and 225.

1.2. Poverty

Whilst the proportion of those in absolute poverty is falling, the actual numbers are still rising due to high rates of population growth in low-income countries; the 1992 UNFPA (United Nations Fund for Population Activities) report showed a fall from 52% in 1970 to 44% by 1985 in the proportion but an

Number of poor (million)

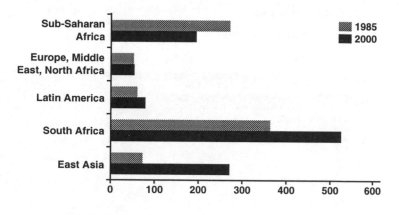

NB: Figure for 1985 projected to 2000.
Source: World Bank World development report, 1990, p.5.

increase from 944 to 1,156 million in the numbers. The balance sheet on human development in Annex 2, produced by the UNDP, assesses more generally the progress made to date.

Forecasts on the number of poor in 2000 (shown below) show a regionally diverse picture of poverty. In this scenario, poverty in sub-Saharan Africa could account for more than 30% of the developing countries' poor by 2000, as against 16% in 1985.[5] Alternative projections based on slower growth and policies less favourable to the poor show an additional 150 million poor, mainly in India.

Food security problems already affect over 1 billion people and are predicted to become more acute, despite the fact that globally there will be enough food for the rising world population. Poverty in low-income countries is at its worst in the rural areas and shows no sign of abating, whilst that of urban areas is on the increase.

One particular trend is towards what the Dutch development report refers to as the 'feminization of poverty'. Due to the vulnerable position of women in the economy and the complexity of their tasks and roles within the household, recession and the disappearance of a number of basic social amenities under structural adjustment programmes have disproportionately affected them.

More generally, there is a trend of increasing inequality in living conditions in the world. In income terms alone, the richest 20% of the world's population are estimated to have received some 60 times more than the bottom 20% by 1990 (compared with 30 times in 1960). Taking disparities at national level into account, the gaps are even larger.[6] Increasing gaps in the levels of human development frustrate the chances of many developing countries to compete in world markets and 'catch up'.

2. GLOBAL CHALLENGES PRESENTED BY POVERTY AND POPULATION GROWTH

The poverty outlined above relates with other factors to present a series of challenges for these societies and the wider global system to deal with. The challenges from disease, drugs and migration are highlighted below.

2.1. Disease

Poor access to education and health services not only encourages high levels of fertility and infant mortality but helps the spread of diseases, especially when poor standards of living and levels of nutrition compound the situation. Infectious parasitic and diarrhoeal diseases continue to account for 45% of all the cases of mortality in the developing world, despite gains in reducing the rate itself. Contaminated drinking water and poor sanitation cause 62% of all deaths in sub-Saharan Africa. Rising worldwide rates of HIV infection will have a major social and economic impact, particularly among the worst hit countries, with 600,000 deaths from AIDS having so far been reported worldwide.[7]

2.2. The drug trade

The value of illicit drugs sold in the USA and Europe has been estimated at USD 122 billion in 1989.[8] This internationally specialized trade generates such huge amounts of hard currency that drug traffickers can act as central bankers in several countries. It is estimated that in the USA alone 60% of commercial banks handle drug money.[9] The drug trade is an acute social problem with global ramifications due to the complex linkages between areas of supply and demand. Thus strategies must address all sides of the problem: law enforcement, money laundering, political linkages, demand, trafficking, drug production and alternative sources of income. Indeed, if such strategies are to be effective, they must tackle wider structural questions such as the situation of farmers within these regions, drug consumption and the political establishment.

2.3. Migration and refugees

People move when there are large differences of relative income to act as a magnet, when there is unemployment, depravity, poverty, squalor and the absence of opportunities. The first major trend to recognize is rural-urban migration due to the lack of opportunities in rural areas. On average, between 20 and 30 million people move to the towns every year; one projection estimates an increase in the proportion of Third World populations living in towns from 17% in 1950 to 46% by 2010.[10] Developing country cities as a group will grow by 160% over this period, whereas rural populations will grow by only 10%. By 2000, there will be 21 megacities in the world with more than 10 million inhabitants and 17 will be in developing countries.

Migration is not normally an irrational flight to the first major metropolis or port. It usually occurs on a chain principle with information, money[11] and people flowing along established lines. However, famines, natural disasters, political repression and war can cause migratory shocks; for example, the Gulf War alone displaced 2.8 million people in a matter of months, the figures for the former Yugoslavia being similar.

In the short term, the principal challenge for the North and Europe in particular comes from these migratory shocks, given the political, economic and environmental tensions in the surrounding regions. In the longer term, migration levels will be distinctly influenced by demographic and economic disparities in the regions surrounding the European Community and compounded by high rates of unemployment, unfavourable agricultural options and limited water resources. The graph below[12] shows population pressure to the south of the EC is set to rise. However, the decline in Western Europe's population may generate demand for migrant labour in the longer run.[13]

With regard to the current decade J. C. Chesnais and C. Seibel foresee an extra 1 million immigrants per year for the EC as a whole in the next decade.[14] With regard to Eastern Europe and the CIS, migratory flows will depend upon the containment of ethnic tensions and whether or not economic reforms take hold. The magnitude of the dangers can be seen from the catastrophe in the former Yugoslavia, where more than three million people have already been displaced.

Migration also represents a brain drain as it is often the most skilled or educated who move to where they see opportunities. Taking figures from the UNDP, by 1987 Africa had lost nearly one third of its skilled people. More than removing skilled people, this emigration also reduces developing countries capacity to train and pass on knowledge to a new generation of professionals, a task which increasingly falls to expensive foreign experts.[15]

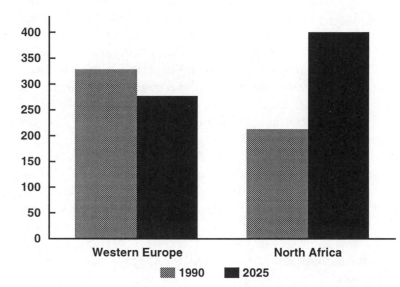

Projected population 1990 and 2025 (million)

Western Europe   North Africa

▨ 1990   ■ 2025

Cumulative international migration, 1990–2015
(assuming economic stagnation in the regions of origin)[1]

From	To		*(million people)*
	North America	Western Europe	Total
CIS	1.8	4.2	6.0
Central Europe	0.9	2.1	3.0
Africa	1.5	3.5	5.0
Middle East	0.9	2.1	3.0
Total	5.0	12.0	17.0

[1] 'Scanning the future. A long-term study of the world economy', 1992, p. 225. The figures are based on the global shift and global crisis scenarios of the authors. 'In the global shift and global crisis scenarios, the regions of origin (Africa, Middle East, Central Europe and the CIS) are characterized by economic stagnation', p. 225.

3. THE ENVIRONMENTAL CHALLENGE: BETWEEN THE SCYLLA OF RISING POVERTY AND THE CHARYBDIS OF OVERCONSUMPTION

'It is futile to deal with environmental problems without broader perspectives that encompass the factors underlying world poverty and international inequality.'[16]

Without the necessary means and security for survival, poor people and countries have little choice but to overuse and destroy their natural resources resulting in ecological deterioration and a sacrifice of the future to salvage the present. Even when poverty is not a cause of environmental decline, it is a ticket to suffer the environmental abuses caused by archaic production methods.[17]

On the other hand, most global environmental threats, from groundwater contamination to climate change, are the by-products of affluence.[18] This is illustrated by the fact that per capita consumption of energy from fossil fuels is 33 times higher in the USA than in India and 10 times higher in the OECD than developing countries on average. If the North continues in its present pattern of resource consumption and the developing world follows the same historical pattern and approaches these northern patterns, then the world's ecological balance is likely to change dramatically with only partly foreseeable consequences.

Economic growth rates (for the world) have remained constant at around 3% since 1950. If they continue at this rate, then the world economy will be five times larger in the year 2050 than it is now, by which date the population of the world is projected to have doubled.[19] The critical question then is: how can natural resource use and the ecological damage of production practices be limited, whilst substantially improving the standards of living of the poorest 1 billion of the world's population and providing adequate conditions for the projected

5.7 billion extra people who will join the world by the year 2050? In order to provide a clearer picture of the order of magnitude underlying this question, some of the major global challenges to the world's environment on the basis of the continuation of current patterns are outlined below.

3.1. Atmospheric pollution

Current economic behaviour is altering the precarious balance of atmospheric gases which make life on earth possible. In cumulative terms, the rich countries are responsible for more than 90% of the increase in greenhouse gases.[20] The size of this greenhouse effect remains unclear but the best estimate of the International Panel on Climatic Change shows a rise in temperature of 3°C by the end of the next century under a business as usual scenario.[21] The possible alteration of climatic zones could have profound effects on ecologies, societies, economies, agricultural ecosystems and water supplies.

The future trends in energy consumption, shown below, will play a central role in this process. The projected energy consumption increases in the developing world could be offset to some extent by the development of new renewable energy technology and energy-saving techniques if appropriate policy measures are taken by these countries and the North. The overall responsibility of the OECD remains clear not only because it will still represent the largest energy consumption share in 2005, but also because it is largely responsible for the historical concentration of greenhouse gases.

Pollution of the air itself is also a problem the world over. An estimated 1.3 billion people worldwide live in urban areas not meeting World Health Organization (WHO) standards.[22]

Primary energy demand by world region[1]

Region	1990 Million toe	% share	2005 Million toe	% share
OECD	4,112	50	4,935	44
Former Soviet Union	1,359	16	1,581	14
Central and Eastern Europe	366	4	415	4
Developing world	2,459	30	4,210	38
World	8,295	100	11,141	100

[1] European Commissison, 'Energy in the future – A view to the future', September. 1992, p. 51.

3.2. Water pollution and degradation of the marine environment

Rising industrial, agricultural and domestic demand for water is chasing a declining and increasingly polluted supply. Consumption is outstripping supplies in northern China and consumption could reach crisis proportions in the Middle East and North Africa.

With regard to world fish stocks, the Food and Agriculture Organization (FAO) estimates that four of the world's 17 major marine fishing areas are overfished.[23] Coastlines are not exempt from pollution, as countries develop them for urban, commercial and industrial uses. Available figures indicate that most tropical countries have lost more than one half of their coastal mangrove forests.[24] Pollution is especially severe in estuaries and enclosed seas, such as the Baltic, Mediterranean and Aral

Sea. In the Mediterranean, the pressure from growing coastal urban populations and a rising number of tourists will pose significant future problems arising from pollution of scarce water supplies and the sea itself.

3.3. Land degradation

Over-intensive land use by the industrial and developing countries is causing serious environmental degradation. Population stress in developing countries often leads to growing energy requirements and pressure to bring more marginal land into agricultural production so leading to deforestation and the loss of biological diversity.[25] Desertification, detectable through satellite imagery, is spreading at a very fast rate in Africa, stripping topsoils and reducing future land use.

With few possibilities to bring new land under cultivation, most observers look to increasing yields rather than expanding the area farmed to increase the quantity of food production. Technological innovations, especially the use of information technology and biotechnology, might transform world agriculture as in the 1960s and 1970s.[26] However, such technology optimism must be tempered with a realization that genetically engineered varieties may have unpredictable effects upon biological diversity and long-term disease resistance.

The actions of landless peasants, mineral speculators, timber firms and the energy needs of developing countries are contributing to a rate of deforestation which has grown from its 1976–80 level of 0.6% per year to 0.9% in the 1980s.[27] If deforestation continues at this rate, further reductions of biological diversity, the displacement of indigenous peoples and a negative impact on the greenhouse effect can be expected. Biological diversity is essential for not only the maintenance of the hydrological cycle and the right balance of atmospheric gases, but also the future productivity of agricultural crops. Decline in genetic diversity at the rate of 4 to 10,000 species every year represents an irreversible decline in the stock of genetic diversity.

3.4. Environmental interdependence

The deep interdependence between the developing and industrialized nations based on the exploitation of a common ecosystem is at the core of the development and environment debate. It is complicated by the lack of precise knowledge about the effect of our actions upon environmental processes.

However, it is clear that nations face a complex web of ecological problems extending beyond their national borders, that present growing regional and global security threats. Environmental migration has already been recognized as a problem and will increase as climatic changes destabilize still further ecologically marginal communities. A future rise in world sea levels would cause immense problems in low-lying areas of both the South and North, with parts of Western Europe particularly at risk. Thus the first challenge that irreversible environmental change will pose will be to the ability of governments to cope with the human costs associated with such radical alterations of the natural environment. Although fears of resource wars may be exaggerated, it seems probable that tension over disputed natural resources (e.g. water in the Middle East) will rise. Trade sanctions for environmental reasons which could result in trade wars are already on the international agenda. Thus the world could be facing major future crises in the near to medium term over the management of change in, and access to, the environments resources.

4.   ECONOMIC OUTLOOK: DIVERSE FUTURES, FRAGILE HOPES

The deep trends outlined in the previous section will be influenced by the prospects for economic growth in developing countries and the wider world economy. The future economic performance of developed and developing countries will condition their ability to shift to sustainable development paths.

The 1990s began badly for developing countries with aggregate real GDP per capita declining in the first two years. Globally, economic recovery is not just a political priority for the OECD, but an economic necessity for many developing countries. A 1% increase in OECD growth sustained over three years is projected to raise developing countries exports by USD 60 billion.[28]

Reading from the economic projections for developing regions to 2000 and beyond (see box), it is clear that the divergence in their performances will continue. Worse still, the marginalization of a greater number of the world's population appears likely.

Regionally, sub-Saharan Africa is likely to experience further stagnation if not regression, as economic growth rates struggle to keep pace with population growth. Prospects in the Middle East and North Africa depend upon political stability, the continuation of economic reforms and the containment of tensions. Latin America is expected to arrest its economic stagnation, although it will experience considerable variation in relative economic performance.

An analysis of comparative strengths among the world's regions shows that Latin America and Africa have a slight advantage in only 3 of 12 central driving forces, namely natural resources, incentives/property rights and individual adaptability. Otherwise they are deficient in their savings rates, price formation, autonomy of the economic sphere, invention and innovation, collective adaptability, cooperation, quality of government, infrastructure and education.[29] Eastern Europe is perhaps the hardest region for which to make forecasts. However, both the Centre d'études prospectives et d'informations internationales (CEPII) and the World Bank predict that if the economic reform plans are implemented then there may be

Economic projections for the period to 2000 and beyond (I)	
	Centre d'études prospectives et d'informations internationales[1]
Sub-Saharan Africa	Improved performance in 1990s. Although the problem of debt (17 African countries fall into the category of severely indebted) might be resolved by the end of the century, that of the finance of development will certainly not. GNP growth rate of 3.1% (1990–95) and 3.5% (1995–2000). Stagnation predicted.
Latin America	Better economic growth than in the 1980s. The relatively good performance of some countries in the region will mask the poor performance of the others. GNP growth rate of 3.0% (1990–95) and 3.8% (1995–2000).
East Asia	In a rather lifeless international environment, only the Asiatic zone should be able to pursue a path of rapid growth. South-East Asia should harvest the benefits of progress from its international insertion and the advantages of a dynamic regional environment. GNP growth rate of 6.4% (1990–95) and 7.0% (1995–2000) for the four Asian NICs.
Eastern Europe	Two phases. 1990–94: A first phase of transition in which the effects of moving away from the central planning system adversely affect the economy with a deep fall in industrial output and balance-of-payments problems. International aid (4% of GNP in Central and Eastern Europe and 1.5% of GNP in the former Soviet Union) predicted. GNP growth of −1.7% (1990–95). 1995–2000: A progressive move back into growth determined principally by the rate that the residual stock of old equipment is downgraded and the flow of new investment. GNP growth rate of 2.6% (1995–2000).

79

Middle East and North Africa	With an increased savings ratio and economic reforms leading to a better mobilization of these investment resources, the region's GNP is expected to grow at 3.5% (1990–95) and by 4.0% (1995–2000). However, the main obstacles to growth remain the increase in population and the political tensions generated in the reform process, which will continue to make investors hesitant.
South Asia	The availability of cheap capital will be the crucial factor in this region in the coming decade, along with the progression of the reform processes. Figures for GNP growth contained in the rest of Asia figure of 5.8% (1990–95) and 6.8% (1995–2000).

[1] Centre d'études prospectives et d'information internationales, 'Économie mondiale 1990–2000: L'impératif de croissance', 1992, pp. 14, 260, 309, 311, 313, 314, 361.

Economic projections for the period to 2000 and beyond (II)

	World Bank[1]	Central Planning Bureau[2]
Sub–Saharan Africa	Economic reforms in several countries expected to raise region's GDP growth to 3.5%. Not high enough to keep pace with population growth. Growth of GDP per capita 0.3% p.a.	GDP growth rates range from 2.9 to 4.9% (1990–2015) under the CPBs four scenarios of global crisis, balanced growth, European Renaissance and global shift. Labour supply to grow by between 3 and 3.4% in same time period.
Latin America	Latin America's economic performance will improve sharply, based on a continued resolution of the debt crisis and a significant shift toward market-friendly policies. GDP growth rate of 4.2%. Per capita, 2.2%.	GDP growth rates from 2.8 to 5.6% under CPBs scenarios (1990–2015). Labour supply, 1.8 to 2.1%.
East Asia	East Asia is unlikely to repeat its impressive economic performance of the past decade; nevertheless, it will remain the fastest-growing developing region, and per capita incomes are projected to rise at a rate of over 5% per year. GDP growth rate of 7.1% projected. Per capita, 5.7%.	GDP growth rates from 6 to 7.3% under CPBs four scenarios (1990–2015). Labour supply, 1.5 to 1.7%.
Eastern Europe	Prospects for growth in Eastern Europe and the	GDP growth rates from 1.6% to 2.7%. (1990–

	former Soviet Union are highly uncertain, but if commitment to economic reforms remains steadfast, the economies of the region can be expected to stabilize in the near future, laying the basis for recovery and growth in the remainder of the decade. Projected GDP growth rate of 1.9%. Per capita, 1.6% for decade (14.2% in 1991).	2015). Labour supply, 0.5 to 0.6%
Middle East & North Africa	Region was adversely affected by the Gulf War. However, it is expected to average 4.5% GDP growth, most of this growth being concentrated in the second half of the decade. This assumes that economic reforms initiated in the region will continue. Per capita GDP growth rate, 1.6%.	GDP growth rates from 3.2 to 3.8% (1990–2015). Labour supply, 3 to 3.3%.
South Asia	Structural reforms in the major South Asian economies will serve to keep aggregate GDP per capita growth at around 3% a year, near the rate achieved in the 1980s. Per capita GDP growth rate, 3.1%.	GDP growth rates from 4.5 to 6.5% (1990–2015). Labour supply, 1.4 to 1.7%.

1   World Bank, 'Global economic prospects and the developing countries 1992', pp. 1, 2, 10 and 11.
2   Netherlands Central Planning Bureau, 'Scanning the future. A long term study of the world economy' 1992, pp. 187, 194, 200 and 204.

a move back to growth after 1995. While the prospects for most developing regions look fragile, the buoyant Asian–Pacific area seems set to continue its integration into the world economy and remain the most economically dynamic region in the immediate future.

4.1. Factors influencing these forecasts

In addition to the deep trends in population growth, poverty and environmental degradation, a number of other factors, which are listed below, could influence these economic forecasts.

(a) Access to capital

In the 1990s, access to investment resources may prove to be problematic due to the northern economies' growing needs, for example for financing budget deficits (in particular in the USA and Germany) and economic growth. The North then may well continue to drain the lion's share of world savings, whilst the competition for what remains will become fiercer as the East European economies' demand for capital spirals upwards and the Gulf region reconstructs its economies and Germany needs to cover the rising costs of unification. With real interest rates remaining high, investment resources will remain costly and debt repayments high for severely indebted countries.

(b) Market access

Developing countries face a volatile trading situation, with no assurance of increased access to northern markets. It has been estimated that a 50% reduction in EC, Japanese and US trade barriers could raise developing countries' exports by USD 50 billion.[30] Clearly an open and fair trading system is essential for the future of developing countries' economies, although some

83

may experience negative side-effects from greater trade liberalization in the short to medium term (notably in sub-Saharan Africa).

(c) Demand pull from industrial countries

Developing countries' growth has been closely linked to growth in manufacturing exports. The influence this will have upon developing countries will depend upon the import elasticity of demand for their products. So without diversification away from agricultural products and commodities for which demand is relatively inelastic, developing countries (especially in sub-Saharan Africa) will find it difficult to increase their export revenues. For instance, it will be the more dynamic manufacturing exporters who will, along with European companies, benefit from the removal of internal barriers, scale economies and the free movement of factors which the single market provides. Overall, the single market is not estimated to have a major impact in trading terms on developing countries – the trade creation and trade diversion effects may cancel each other out. However, some investment diversion effects at the expense of third countries have been projected.[31]

(d) The avoidance of energy shocks

Similar quantum increases in energy and oil prices to those which aggravated worldwide recessions in 1974/75 and 1980/81 would hurt, in particular, the poorest developing countries.

(e) Peace dividends and political stability

The containment of ethnic, nationalist and religious tensions will be crucial in securing a stable climate for economic rejuvenation and the realization of peace dividends. These could be important not only for the NATO countries and the former Warsaw Pact which account for 80% of world military expenditure, but also for developing countries whose spending as a percentage of GNP is sometimes very high (see graph below). Whilst military expenditure declined by 3.0% world-wide between 1987 and 1990, the expected massive cutbacks, which could yield some USD 1.5 trillion by 2000,[32] have yet to materialize. Without a stable geopolitical climate, restructuring of arms industries in both North and South and reduction of arms trade, this potential will remain largely unfulfilled.

Military expenditure as a percentage of GNP in 1987

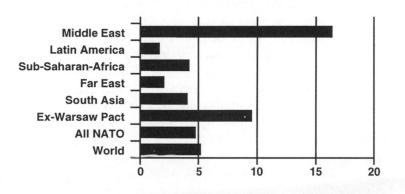

(f) Adjustment to globalization

In the longer term, the prospects of developing countries depend upon their relationship with the deep trend towards globalization in the world economy and, in particular, in world trade. Those outside or peripheral to these processes of globalization and regional integration in the northern economies have tended to lose ground. Efforts to update or create a modern infrastructure, develop a modern skilled and educated workforce, and integrate technology and know-how in

85

production processes are crucial future competitiveness vectors. For those countries on the peripheries, which are not well integrated into the world trading and without niche markets and some system comparative advantage, times are likely to be very tough because the competitive 'ante' conditions in order to participate are becoming ever more stringent.

5.   SCENARIOS FOR THE FUTURE

5.1.   Business as usual scenario

In the table below, possible implications of a scenario of a continuation of certain current trends are sketched in terms of some of the principal risks for the world as a whole, and the European Community in particular. It is, of course, extremely difficult if not impossible to attach probabilities to any of these outcomes. There will be unpredictable shocks which the current system may be unable to manage (natural catastrophes and conflicts of variable intensity and duration) and positive surprises. However, the weight of expected bad outcomes under business as usual scenarios should be of sufficient concern to urge alternative and new approaches.

Extrapolation of the status quo trend	Risks for North and South
Over 5.8 billion people by the year 2050	• Large increase in poverty and starvation • Further environmental destruction • Possible epidemics/new diseases • Mass migration pressures • Deepening North–South alienation, possible conflicts • Greater competition for natural resources and primary energy sources, driving their prices
Environmental destruction continues	• Irreversible change in the ecosystem with incalculable costs • Changes in climatic zones with negative effects on agricultural production • Desertification/water shortage/sea-level rise/species loss • Accelerated migration • Violation of the rights of future generations • Increased propensity for conflict over scarce resources
Slow economic growth in LDCs	• Maintenance of indebtedness and threats to stability of the world financial system • Inability to eradicate poverty and redress the unfair distribution of income • Underdevelopment of huge new markets • Inability to attract private FDI for LDCs • Unending pressures to accelerate development aid to the South with the Community, for reasons of proximity and history in the front line • Increased competition for aid funds (South versus East) • Greater numbers of migrants

Political systems in LDCs remain unresponsive to the needs for change	• Perseverance of substantial outflows of corrupt capital • Proliferation of the supply of drugs • LDCs maintain excessive levels of military expenditure and purchase a share of the hardware from the EC • Confrontational North-South politics remain • Increasing social tensions within the LDCs and in the North due to rising immigration leading to the danger of escalating racism • Investments in LDCs remain high risk and technology transfer minimal • Economic progress in the South paralysed
Unchanged military expenditure in the North, South and East	• Dangers of nuclear proliferation and diffusion of weapons of mass destruction • Enhanced probability of conflicts and environmental destruction • Scrabbling among northern arms producers to sell in the South • The potential of an unlimited quantity of uprooted refugees

5.2. A gradual change to a sustainable future scenario

In the second scenario, the consequences of shifting social, economic and political policies on to a more sustainable basis are highlighted. The central conclusion is that the long-run benefits of such policies will lessen the probability of the worst case scenario and, *ceteris paribus*, lead to substantial benefits. It is a positive sum game.

These two opposing scenarios offer contrasting visions of the future. The first entails risks and the bottling-up of future problems. The real issue is whether these risks are worth taking. This report, like many before, argues that they are not. The expected gains of policy adjustments towards sustainability criteria will certainly outweigh the costs. This requires from politicians long-term vision and the courage to lead and convince public opinion on the need for some sacrifice to offset the imminent risks and dangers building up. Without such vision, history's judgment of our generation may be severe.

Sustainable development	Possible gains
Sustainable population levels and reduction of poverty	• Decreased migratory pressure • More manageable levels of poverty to address • Less pressure on natural resources • Lower consumption of environmental capital • Lower chances of conflict • Opportunity to re-equilibrate distribution of income
Protecting environmental capital through sustainable development policies	• Diminished chance of irreversible ecological damage • Respecting intergenerational equity • Improved long-run economic performance • Contribution to reducing poverty (e.g. by protecting water resources)
Accelerated, but sustainable economic growth paths in developing countries	• Reducing Third World indebtedness and global financial risks • Progressive LDC integration in the world economy and new market opportunities in the South for the North • Reduced migratory pressure • Private-sector capital flows develop to the South • Diversification of economies • Increased North-South cooperative efforts on alternative energies • Availability of capital to maintain environmental and social projects
Reforming political systems (governance)	• Reduction of waste, corruption • Optimal chance for long-run political and social stability • Reduction of military expenditure, drugs • Decrease in refugees/migrants • Essential trigger for economic progress

	• Political integration into new world order of governance • New opportunities for global partnership and cooperation
Reduced military expenditure and arms trade	• Decrease in global security threats • More optimal allocation of world resources, capital and labour • Decreased propensity for local conflicts • Fewer refugees

Notes

1 See, in particular, the World Bank World development reports of 1990, 1991, and 1992; World Bank reports 'Global economic prospects and the developing countries', 1991 and 1992; the UNDP Human development reports, 1990, 1991 and 1992; The Dutch Government report 'A world of difference – A new framework for development cooperation in the 1990s', 1991; the Netherlands Central Planning Bureau report 'Scanning the future. A long-term study of the world economy', 1992; the report of the Centre d'études prospectives et d'informations internationales 'Économie mondiale 1990–2000: L'impératif de croissance', 1992; 'World resources 1992–93 – Towards sustainable development – A guide to the global environment', 1992; the OECD report 'Long-term prospectives of the world economy', 1992; communication of the European Commission 'Development cooperation in the run-up to 2000', 15 May 1992.

2 The less-optimistic predictions suggest figures of upwards of 15 billion people. World development report, 1992, p. 26.

3 Human development report, 1992, p. 14.

4 Education, particularly of women, is a powerful cause of reduced fertility; netting out other important factors such as income, a secondary education compared with three years of primary education reduces the number of children born to a woman from seven to four. World development report, 1992, p. 29.

5 World development report, 1990, p. 5.

91

6 Developing countries as a whole account for 77.1% of the world population but only 15.8% of global GNP and 19.3% of world trade. Human development report, 1992, p. 37.

7 Over half the 5 to 10 million infected people are estimated to live in sub-Saharan Africa. It is also spreading rapidly through Asia, the Asian Development Bank estimating that by 2000 the majority of the 40 million HIV infections and 10 million adult AIDS cases worldwide will be in Asia.

8 See European Parliament Report on the spread of organized crime linked to drugs trafficking in the Member States of the European Community, 1992.

9 *Ibidem.*

10 Nothcott, Jim and Christie, Ian. 'Shaping factors and business strategies in the post-1992 European Community', paper by the UK's Policy Studies Institute, April, 1992.

11 In 1989, developing countries received around USD 25 billion in official remittances. Human development report, 1992, p. 56.

12 Figures from Bertelsmann Foundation 'Challenges in the Mediterranean – The European response', Research Group on European Affairs, 1991, p. 11.

13 See 'Population trends and Europe', report of the Forward Studies Unit of the European Commission, 1990.

14 Chesnais, Jean-Claude and Seibel, Claude. *L'évolution socio-démographique: Éléments prospectifs.*

15 Research suggests this figure is as high as 150,000 foreign experts. Van Dam, F. 'Noord-Zuid balans van veertig jaar' in *Internationale Spectator*, June 1992 .

16 Brundtland report, 'Our common future'.

17 Dunning, Allan B. 'Poverty and the environment: Reversing the downward spiral', Worldwatch Paper 92, 1989, pp. 40–54.

18 *Ibidem*, p. 40.

19 'Scanning the future. A long-term study of the world economy', 1992, p.123.

20 'A world of difference. A new framework for development cooperation in the 1990s', 1991, p. 73.

21 World development report, 1992, p. 7.

22 World development report, 1992, p. 5.

23 The Mediterranean, the Pacific coast off Latin America, the

Pacific coast of Japan and the eastern coasts of the Indian Ocean. FAO, 'Recent developments in world fisheries', April 1991.

24 'World resources 1992–93 – Towards sustainable development – A guide to the global environment', 1992, p. 175.

25 Research by the International Soil Reference and Information Centre in the Netherlands has shown that about 1,200 million hectares of land worldwide are degraded as a result of improper agricultural management and grazing. Oldeman, L.R., Hakkeling, R.T.A and Somebroek, W.G., 'World map of the status of human-induced soil degradation – An explanatory note', ISRIC, Waginingen, 1991.

26 Brown, Martin and Goldin, Ian. 'The future of agriculture: Developing country implications', OECD Development Centre, 1992.

27 Asia's deforestation rate is the highest at 1.2% per year for 1981–90, Latin America is second with 0.9% and Africa a close third with 0.8%. 'World resources 1992–93 – Towards sustainable development – A guide to the global environment', 1992, p. 118.

28 World Bank, 'Global economic prospects and the developing countries', 1992, p. 2.

29 'Scanning the future. A long-term study of the world economy', 1992, p. 182.

30 In 1991 prices. See 'Global economic prospects and the developing countries', 1992, p. 3.

31 See World Bank 'The impact of EC-92 on developing countries' trade: A dissenting view' International Economics Department, 1992 and Davenport, Michael and Page, Sheila. 'Europe 1992 and the developing world', Overseas Development Institute, 1991.

32 Human development report, 1992, p. 86.

Chapter IV

A global strategy for the promotion of sustainable economic and social development

The preceding chapters have shown that there is an increasing need and perhaps a window of opportunity for strengthening multilateralism in order to define and implement more coherent global strategies for sustainable development. First, the changed geopolitical situation resulting in the end of bipolar hegemony provides both new opportunities for stability and new risks of conflicts, contradictions and tensions which are ideally handled multilaterally. The European Community, in view of its economic strength, political weakness and strategic vulnerability should have a particularly strong interest in promoting better global management of interdependence within multilateral frameworks. Second, the disappearance of ideological confrontation in global East-West and North-South relations has contributed to a greater convergence of thinking about the conditions for development and the shortcomings of governance at the domestic and international level. This should facilitate overcoming apparent short-term conflicts of interests in favour of globally beneficial longer-term strategies agreed in multilateral frameworks. Third, an increasing awareness of the

95

deep global trends of population growth, rising poverty and depletion of natural resources which can be expected to result in increased migratory pressures, environmental threats and other global security risks provides incentives for more vigorous initiatives at the international level to modify the patterns of development. In sum, governments should now be in a better position to respond more adequately to the global challenges.

However, this requires their readiness to assume responsibility for the internal and external long-term consequences of their policies, their acceptance of the challenge of globalization in terms of more effective global management of interdependencies and a commitment to a comprehensive approach towards the promotion of sustainable economic and social development worldwide. Following the clarification of the conceptual basis in this sense, the chapter outlines a number of strategic orientations in terms of promoting deep integration, stimulating sustainable economic growth, reorienting development towards environmental sustainability and establishing long-term development contracts between donors and poor countries. The chapter finally contains some ideas for the transformation and strengthening of international institutions.

1. THE CONCEPTS OF GOOD GOVERNANCE, GLOBAL GOVERNANCE AND SUSTAINABLE DEVELOPMENT

1.1. Good governance: an enlightened self-interest

After decades of blaming the colonial heritage or the northern domination of an unjust international economic system for most of their problems, developing countries now increasingly accept that development depends primarily on the policies they adopt and implement. The fundamental elements of policy orientation and good governance of developing countries in the

South or East are thus becoming part of a more and more universal *acquis*. While elites and pressure groups in many developing countries still resist necessary changes, they are no longer protected by a benevolent superpower and face increasing pressures from both their own populations and the international community to face up to their responsibilities.

The problems of good governance of the industrialized countries in terms of the external and boomerang effects of their policies are not as clearly recognized. Under pressure from electorates defending a privileged way of life and strong special interest groups seeking economic advantages, Western democracies have so far proven incapable of living up to the standards of good behaviour which their leaders preach to others. The Western rhetoric about the benefits of free trade and division of labour is thus contradicted by the many trade distortions and market access restrictions facing products of developing countries whenever they have gained, or are about to gain, comparative advantages. The insistence of representatives of affluent societies on the necessity of protecting the global environment and fighting poverty is not matched by adequate efforts to reduce energy consumption and share resources more equitably. Presently, the international community disposes of insufficient means to induce industrialized countries to modify their policies in the interest of global welfare.

In the present international climate of economic slowdown, distrust of established leaderships and re-emergence of strong nationalist, ethnocentric, fundamentalist and inward-looking currents, decisive progress towards the assumption of shared responsibilities for global problems may appear unrealistic.

However, industrialized countries are becoming increasingly aware of the consequences of incoherent policies and inaction in terms of mounting risks threatening the security of their own populations as a result, in particular, of eruptions of violence, migratory pressures and ecological catastrophes. The end of hegemonic bipolarity has reduced the possibility of imposing solutions unilaterally and shown that splendid isolation behind a protected fortress is an unrealistic option in an interdependent world. It is therefore increasingly a matter of self-interest for northern countries to reorient their policies and initiate new global strategies for the solution of global problems.

1.2. Global governance: a concept of managing interdependencies

The world economy has long been characterized by a trend towards globalization driven primarily by international companies pursuing planetary strategies and accelerated by the technological developments and deregulation of international markets, more recently in the financial and monetary area. Economic globalization means rapid diffusion of innovations around the world and translates into higher growth rates for trade than for production and, in particular, rapid growth of foreign direct investment. Economic globalization, therefore, potentially offers better opportunities for rapid development than in the past.

An important effect of globalization is that economic development is increasingly difficult, if not impossible, outside the world economy. Economic isolationism and *de facto* marginalization mean losing access to new technologies and financial resources, diminishing competitiveness and forgoing developmental possibilities. The collapse of the communist bloc which had fallen far behind in key technological evolutions demonstrates this as much as the failure of autonomous and inward-looking development strategies pursued in parts of the southern hemisphere. Resisting the process of globalization is therefore quixotic and suicidal for any country. Countries are better advised to adapt to this inevitable process and adopt development strategies which allow them to participate in the world economy and benefit from globalization.

However, we are also witnessing a globalization of risks

resulting from market failures and other systemic shortcomings. Rising inequalities and structural poverty, environmental degradation threatening the global ecosystem, uncontrollable drug traffic and arms sales, spread of epidemics and massive migratory movements are, above all, signs of failure of the systems of government at all levels and of a crisis in international relations.

There is thus a rising discrepancy between the globalization of economic opportunities and of societal risks on the one hand, and the evolution of governance on the other. Globalization means that realities at the national level are increasingly influenced by external decisions or events and out of the control of national governments. This does not diminish the crucial role of domestic governments for adequate policies. However, the new interdependencies resulting from globalization require actions at the regional or multilateral level to render domestic policies effective. Bilateral cooperation remains useful in many cases. Nevertheless, with respect to an increasing number of issues, bilateralism can only lead to coherent and lasting solutions if they are embedded and implemented in a multilateral context. Regionalism, at least in the case of the Community, has proven to be the most effective way of dealing with economic interdependence and can be seen as an important phase in facilitating the integration of countries into the world economy while respecting and preserving the diversity of models of development. Regional integration also constitutes an important building block towards coherent global management. However, it is not an alternative to multilateralism. There is even a risk that the absence of effective multilateral disciplines and institutions could lead to the constitution of regional blocs pursuing aggressive or protectionist policies under which developing economies would suffer most.

The fact remains that the trend towards the globalization of economic opportunities and social and environmental risks is not matched by an equally powerful trend towards the globalization of governance in terms of providing political guidance and adequate legal frameworks for the globalization processes. The main reason for this lies in the refusal of governments and electorates – and especially those of relatively powerful countries – to accept the implications of globalization in terms of limiting the traditional concept of sovereignty and requiring solutions on the basis of common reference points rather than mere brokering of national interests. Intergovernmental cooperation at the multilateral level has certainly increased enormously since the war but national bureaucracies and political leaders have generally resisted sharing – responsibility and sovereignty – in the interest of solving common problems and managing interdependencies.

Marginalized Third World populations are those who suffer most from the inadequacy of coherent global governance. However, it is now becoming increasingly evident that the security of developed northern societies is also threatened as a consequence of the absence of adequate responses to the global challenges and risks by the international community. It is, in the first instance, the responsibility of the northern powers which dominate the international system to exercise leadership and take initiatives to guide globalization processes and manage interdependencies and global risks.

The Community, as the living model of integrated governance beyond intergovernmental cooperation, would be best placed to attempt to convince its partners, in particular the USA and Japan, to accept the challenge of globalization in terms of the deeper integration of national policies and the strengthening of global institutions.

Global governance in the post-Yalta era can no longer take the form of an imposition of a dominant model of society in the name of a hegemonic concept of world order. It requires the full respect of cultural diversity in the context of a collective exercise of soft power with respect to the management of interdependencies and global risks. It may imply new forms of conditionality and intervention into what has traditionally been considered the internal affairs of States. However, it must be based on the rule of law and legitimized within fully representative institutional structures. As a consequence, international law will have to be developed considerably.

In the final analysis, assuming global responsibility means the acceptance of the concept of a global society in which each actor has to make his contribution towards the promotion of common welfare and collective security in accordance with such universal values as peace, justice and equity, the protection of human rights, the preservation of the natural environment and respect for cultural diversity.

1.3. Building on a comprehensive concept of sustainable development

The evolution of development thinking, the lessons drawn from the experiences in North-South relations since the war and the analyses of the social, economic and environmental trends suggest that development policies and multilateral strategies must be based on a comprehensive development concept. This concept should encompass, on the one hand, the economic, social, environmental, cultural and political dimensions of development as they interact. It should, on the other hand, cover the interrelationship between internal and external forces, i.e. the interdependence of evolutions at the domestic, regional and global levels. Various recent studies and reports,[1] as well as academic writings reflect a considerable degree of convergence of development thinking. These reports analyse the various dimensions and interdependencies comprehensively without reducing the complexity of challenges, interactions and strategic options to simplistic and ideologically predetermined blueprints.

There are obviously important differences in emphasis and

wording. The 1987 Brundtland Commission report entitled 'Our common future' defines sustainable development as development that 'meets the needs of the present without compromising the ability of future generations to meet their own needs'.[2] The emphasis here is on environmental sustainability in the interest of intergenerational equity. The UNDP uses the concept of sustainable human development defined as 'the process of enlarging the range of people's choice – increasing their opportunities for education, health care, income and employment, and covering the full range of human choices from a sound physical environment to economic and political freedoms'.[3] This definition focuses on the social aspects of development in the spirit of intragenerational equity. The IMF and the OECD's Development Assistance Committee refer to the concept of sustainable economic growth in the context of an analysis of the meso-, macro- and microeconomic conditions for the integration of developing countries into the world economy. The World Bank, in the third of a trilogy of reports looking at poverty (1990), development strategies (1991) and development and environment (1992), has attempted to combine the various elements under the heading of sustained and equitable development.

Negotiators of the Treaty on European Union (Maastricht Treaty) have finally chosen the notion of sustainable economic and social development as the basic objective of development cooperation. This results from Article 130 of the EC Treaty which also contains the objectives of the smooth and progressive integration of developing countries into the world economy and the campaign against poverty as the main poles of a double strategy to achieve the wider goal of sustainable development. According to Article 130u, these objectives have to be taken into account in the context of other Community policies. They also serve for the purpose of coordination with the policies of Members States (Article 130x) and cooperation with third countries and competent international organizations

(Article 130y). The Maastricht Treaty will thus give constitutional quality to a concept of development and development cooperation which is multidimensional in terms of objectives, policies and levels of political action and which seeks policy coherence.

Important divergences of opinion and sometimes bitter controversies also exist and will continue to exist about particular approaches and policies, such as structural adjustment. There remain tensions between economic efficiency, social justice and ecological sustainability which cannot be fully resolved at the theoretical level and, in any event, reflect important conflicts of interest. However, beyond the differences in emphasis, priorities and specific messages, a remarkable convergence of view with respect to analytical parameters, basic concepts and general messages in the various publications can be observed. Moreover, the importance of the concept of sustainable social and economic development does not so much lie in the provision of a blueprint for social, economic, environmental and cooperation policies, but rather in its contribution to the clarification of the full range of issues, conflicts of interest, trade-offs and options. It serves to focus attention on the conditions and the process for making rational choices with respect to the formulation and implementation of coherent long-term development strategies at the domestic as well as at the regional and multilateral levels.

2. STRATEGIC ORIENTATIONS FOR THE PROMOTION OF SUSTAINABLE SOCIAL AND ECONOMIC DEVELOPMENT

It would be futile and counterproductive to attempt to spell out in any detail the global strategies which need to be pursued to reverse the unsustainable deep trends threatening the survival of mankind. They can only result from a coincidence of vision between the major players and a complex process of negotiation. However, the reflections on past experience and prospective evolution of the global system suggest a number of conclusions regarding the strategic orientations which seem to impose themselves if a serious effort to deal with global medium- and long-term problems is to be undertaken.

2.1. Promoting deep economic integration

The lessons from past experience lead to the conclusion that a strategy of deep economic integration through the establishment of more comprehensive regulatory frameworks for economic activities and government policies at the multilateral level would be the adequate response to the challenge of economic globalization in order to reap the full benefits of this natural process and correct global market failures. This should be in the particular interest of weaker countries and economies, which are otherwise left at the mercy of the law of the jungle and risking further marginalization. Such a strategy requires new and stronger multilateral disciplines and rules affecting domestic policies and governmental as well as non-governmental actors in the global economy.

(a)   Towards a comprehensive regulatory framework for trade and investment

The Uruguay Round – focusing in particular on better integration of developing countries into the international trading system, stronger disciplines on agricultural policies, reintegration of textiles and clothing into the GATT, establishment of multilateral rules in the new areas of trade in services and intellectual property protection, strengthening of multilateral dispute-settlement procedures (with the implication of reducing the potential of unilateral pressures and sanctions) as well as the establishment of a multilateral trade organization

(MTO) – will, when concluded, represent a milestone towards a more comprehensive and stronger trading system. However, the results will still be far from constituting a satisfactory and coherent regulatory framework for international trade and investment. In some respects – such as the inclusion of restrictive business practices and commodity agreements – the MTO will not even extend to all areas included in the 1948 Havana Charter for an international trade organization.

In general terms, an adequate response to globalization would consist in promoting deep integration within a multi-lateral framework beyond the traditional forms of liberalization of foreign trade regimes. It would require adequate mechanisms and disciplines for the adjustment of domestic policies regulating economic behaviour. In view of the large and growing number of countries involved in the multilateral context and the differences between them, the method and scope of liberalization, cooperation and integration would obviously be different from those of the Community model. The Community experience which is not limited to the integration of countries at the same level of development, but extended to a relatively successful North–South integration can, however, provide some guidance as to the orientations to be pursued in the global context.

First, market access should be based more on objective criteria and liberalization formula ensuring that economically strong and weak countries alike enjoy the benefits of their comparative advantages and that overly protected countries progressively integrate into the world economy. This would require a shift in traditional methods of bilateral market access negotiations based on negotiating power towards a rule-based approach. In this context, the specific conditions of particular sectors within countries should be taken into account as far as a reasonable level of protection and time-frames for liberalization are concerned. However, no sector should be excluded. Preferential treatment in favour of poor countries should take better account of the characteristics of the products and markets concerned and be limited in time, in accordance with an approach based on the concept of infant industry protection during a transition period.

Second, there should be more emphasis on regulatory convergence, i.e. the approximation if not harmonization of essential public policy requirements at the multilateral level in order to enhance the efficiency of policies protecting common goods, reduce distortions in competition and permit market access on the basis of mutual recognition. The emergence of conflicts between trade and environment policies and the difficulties of liberalizing trade in services both illustrate the orientation of this proposition. However, the standards used in the international context must also reflect differences in the stage of development and should be multilaterally agreed, rather than unilaterally imposed.

Third, a multilateral framework for investment should establish disciplines for domestic investment policies and encourage investment flows and the diffusion of technological know-how. Of particular importance for the stimulation of foreign investment would be the harmonization of prudential, fiscal and accounting regulations in the banking and other financial sectors.

Fourth, the behaviour of private companies operating in international markets should be subject to harmonized rules and enforcement mechanisms. For example, important differences in domestic competition policies or the absence of such policies in many regions of the South entail serious trade distortions, often to the disadvantage of developing economies. In the longer run, an international competition authority should be established.

Fifth, the possibility of coordinated actions to correct conjunctural and structural problems in certain commodity markets should be reconsidered in the light of the failure of most commodity agreements and the characteristics of the goods and markets concerned. In particular, the possibilities of price stabilization through long-term agreements between producers and consumers as well as of reorienting funds targeted for stabilization of export earnings towards diversification and commercial promotion of exports should be examined.

On a more general level, it should be more clearly recognized that free trade is by no means sufficient to achieve sustainable economic and social development. It contributes to an efficient allocation of resources but is of unequal importance in solving the structural problems of the different regions and does not itself provide the solutions for the common goods. Therefore, it will be necessary to interconnect the multilateral trading regime with global monetary, financial and environmental mechanisms in order to ensure policy coherence.

(b)   Strengthening the international monetary and financial mechanisms

The financial cycles and disorder that exist in the monetary and financial system often result in a misallocation of financial resources which jeopardizes economic prospects in both North and South and lead to major outflows of financial resources from developing countries. A strategy that seeks to bring about greater harmony in the global economy must aim to ensure that the developing countries benefit from the globalization of the international monetary and financial system. On this basis, and in the short term, measures should be taken to break the financial cycle and ensure a stable transfer of financial resources to low- and middle-income developing countries, thus helping them to achieve adequate rates of growth.

This would imply, firstly, the stabilization and limitation of debt servicing repayments (principal and interest) to a level compatible with the economic growth of the developing countries concerned, as well as a reduction of the debt stock for the heavily indebted low-income countries. To this effect, existing facilities (e.g. the IDA debt reduction facility) should be strengthened and more ambitious debt reduction initiatives taken in the context of the Paris Club.

Secondly, prudential, fiscal and accounting rules affecting financial operators would need to be improved, for instance by building on the agreements reached in the framework of the Bank for International Settlements and extending them to other financial operators and a maximum number of countries.

Thirdly, the existing arrangements for multilateral monetary cooperation should be strengthened to ensure macroeconomic stability and predictability and provide extra liquidity for countries in adjustment.

In the longer term, the international financial community should provide new regulatory mechanisms to influence international liquidity working both on deficit and surplus countries and smooth out the financial cycle. This could be initiated within the G7 and institutionalized in the IMF.

The World Bank system, and in particular the International Development Agency (IDA) and regional development banks, should be provided with the additional resources needed to enable it to channel more effectively concessional aid and to act as an intermediary between the international financial markets and developing countries, guaranteeing the latter financing on favourable and stable terms. Its advisory and coordinating role with respect to the establishment of and support for adjustment and long-term development strategies should be strengthened. However, developing country representatives should have a greater say in the orientation of the Bank's policies, which must also be better coordinated with the policies of a revitalized United Nations.

2.2. Stimulating sustainable economic growth

The success of the Uruguay Round, the measures designed to break the financial cycle in the short term and the further reforms of the trading, monetary and financial system suggested above will not be enough to ensure adequate rates of growth in the developing countries. Moreover, greater access to the markets of the industrialized countries may be difficult to realize in a period of economic slowdown. Therefore, additional mechanisms that could stimulate sustainable growth in both industrialized and developing countries should be exploited.

As far as the industrialized countries are concerned, coordination of macroeconomic policies through the G7 (and in the long term more representative institutions) should be ameliorated and the implementation of policy recommendations supervised. This concerns, in particular, the establishment and supervision of fiscal and budgetary convergence criteria as well as monetary disciplines in order to bring down interest rates and prevent competitive devaluations. In particular, growth strategies in periods of slowdown need to be better coordinated within the triad. Industrialized countries should also take appropriate measures to avoid additional growth resulting in additional pollution and stimulate investments (e.g. through coordinated fiscal incentives) in environmentally friendly sectors, some of which already have strong growth potentials.

As far as the developing countries are concerned (as well as the countries of Central and Eastern Europe and the CIS), a source of additional economic growth could lie in exploiting the economic relationships between them. It is a question here of placing on a solvent footing the economic relationships between people that account for roughly 85% of mankind and who, up to now, have accounted for less than 25% of world trade. The decline and even collapse of the interregional trade of many of these countries stem, apart from the obvious political factors, from the excessive vertical integration of their economies with industrialized countries and the lack of financial resources that would enable settlement of the trade balances between countries whose currencies are not convertible. The need to secure foreign exchange and the impossibility of granting credit to potential purchasers often condemn these countries to limit trade with one another or to confine themselves to barter operations.

A number of measures could help to strengthen the economic South/South, South/East and East/East links, provided there is a political will for regional cooperation and integration between such countries which is still lacking in many regions, in particular in Africa:

(i)   support for viable regional integration schemes at a political level as well as through economic incentives (e.g. cumulative rules of origin, regionally oriented structural adjustment programmes and development projects, in particular with respect to the establishment of regional infrastructure networks);

(ii) the establishment and financing of a clearing system covering trade between these countries (on the lines of the European Payments Union, which made it possible to revitalize trade in Europe in the post-war years), which could ultimately make their currencies convertible;

(iii) the facilitation of triangular technological cooperation and, more generally, the promotion of interregional technological networking;

(iv) the financing of triangular trade transactions involving two of these countries and an industrialized country.

Finally, the international community could help to overcome some of the major obstacles to private investments in developing countries, such as uncertainties related to the political evolution and prohibitive costs for, in particular, small and medium-sized companies concerning the identification of investment opportunities and the creation of joint ventures. On the one hand, reinsurance schemes to cover foreign investments against political and legal uncertainties at the multilateral level should be reinforced and extended taking the Multilateral Investment Guarantee Agency as a starting point. On the other hand, the development of a multilateral facility along the lines of the ECIP (EC International Investment Partners) could be envisaged.

2.3. Reorienting development towards environmental sustainability

Even though the United Nations Conference on Environment and Development has failed to provide adequate answers to the global threats resulting from the present development trends, important framework conventions (climate change, biodiversity) were signed, principles agreed (Rio Declaration on environment and development, forest principles) and a 500-page programme for action at the local, national and international levels (Agenda 21) adopted. The parameters of a global strategy for the promotion of environmentally sustainable development have thus been established. The challenge lies in proper implementation of the new range of policies outlined. Firstly, this requires convincing recalcitrant countries, regions and local authorities in the North and the South that attaching permanent value to, and protecting, the environment makes economic sense in the medium and long terms, apart from being imperative for security reasons. Secondly, it requires convincing northern countries that it is in their interest to take the lead in terms of modifying their production and consumption patterns and generating resources and technologies that are transferable and that can be equally targeted to help poor countries to attain sustainable development paths. Thirdly, it requires more effective international mechanisms for the integration of the environmental dimension into all areas of policy-making and the coordination of initiatives in order to avoid unreasonable distortions of competition.

Convincing policy-makers and public opinion of the benefits

111

of environmental sustainability requires, in the first instance, a sound knowledge of the ecological costs and benefits of various development patterns and policies. To this effect, comprehensive inventories of natural capital stocks should be established and their evolution systematically monitored. Secondly, cost/benefit calculations of major development projects should include environmental capital, using explicit valuation methodologies. Shadow restoration projects can provide a useful proxy approach for such cost measurements. Thirdly, attempts to draw up 'green' national economic accounts which include the evolution of the natural capital stock should be encouraged to give policy-makers a more accurate real economic barometer for measuring sustainable economic patterns. In addition, information campaigns and an integration of environmental questions in primary and secondary education programmes may help to change the attitudes of all age groups.

Changing unsustainable patterns of behaviour requires primarily appropriate pricing of all goods or services whose production or consumption affects the natural capital stock. In accordance with the 'polluter (or user) pays' principle, this should lead to the progressive integration of environmental externalities into the price system, thereby reflecting, in particular, the scarcity, resilience and non-substitutability of natural resources used. One promising approach in this regard lies in incremental ecological tax reforms leading to progressive price increases for fossil fuels, nuclear power, water, timber, certain minerals, etc. In certain areas, this approach needs to be combined with the establishment of multilaterally agreed quantitative emission, production or consumption limits. In particular, the possibilities of introducing tradable permit mechanisms at the international level should be considered.

A comprehensive sustainability strategy must finally contain important redistributive elements. In view of the discrepancies of consumption patterns between the North and the South, this is not only a question of fairness but of global sustainability and risk prevention. In order to induce developing countries to follow different development patterns in terms of the consumption of non-renewable natural resources, significant transfers of resources combined with technological know-how will be necessary in economic transition phases. This concerns, in particular, the provision of clean water, sanitation, locally produced food crops, new and renewable energy sources (wind, solar, biomass), energy-saving techniques and collective public transport systems. New forms of technological cooperation, including the financing of North/South and South/South joint ventures and regional cooperation projects and the encouragement of decentralized technological networking, have to play a much more important role in this context. This requires additional financial resources for poor countries, which can only in part be provided through a reorientation of existing assistance policies or debt rescheduling and forgiving techniques (such as debt for nature swaps). The Global Environment Facility (GEF) will have to be considerably increased if these long-run aims are to be achieved. Ideally, these funds should come from international energy and pollution taxes.

2.4. Supporting sustainable development in poor countries through development contracts

Development cooperation has evolved from bilateral and mostly tied aid conditioned largely by geopolitical considerations to structural adjustment loans conditioned by rigid economic reform policies. To be effective, cooperation and assistance presuppose a supportive domestic environment and policies which are credible in terms of orientation, political backing and capacity of implementation. In the longer term, success depends on whether domestic (local, national, regional) authorities establish development strategies corresponding to socio-economic realities and make them work. Donors, rather than imposing solutions unilaterally, should concentrate on

113

giving adequate policy advice and reaching agreement on a coherent policy framework with the recipient country. This, in turn, requires more structured efforts of coordination and consensus-building among donors at the source and on the spot than in the past, where such exercises were more sporadic, limited to the Bretton Woods institutions and a few like-minded donors, and generally lacking a serious policy dialogue with the recipient country.

This process could lead towards quasicontractual long-term relations of partnership between, on the one hand, individual or regional groupings of developing countries involving also non-governmental organizations in these countries, and, on the other hand, the major donors including governments, international agencies and non-governmental organizations. The reward for such a cumbersome process of establishing development contracts should be more predictability and increased confidence in development strategies which actually work in a sustainable manner.

The development contracts, building on the experience gained under both the Lomé Convention and the policy framework programmes (PFPs) and letters of development policy/intent of the World Bank and the IMF, should contain flexible policy frameworks adjusted to the particular situation of the individual countries. They should avoid imposing a particular model of society and fully respect cultural diversity. In the light of the lessons drawn from past experience (Chapter II.2), these contractual agreements would, however, need to contain certain commitments by recipient countries concerning the respect of basic human rights, fundamental liberties, the rule of law, participatory political structures and social, economic, environmental and administrative reform programmes (including, for instance, the orientation of budgetary expenditure towards human development priorities). They should also contain commitments by donor countries with respect to specific policy instruments affecting the recipient countries, such as GSP (generalized system of preferences) status, debt alleviation and concessional aid. Their aim would be to ensure secure financial and technical support for policies ranging from family planning, development of human resources and capacity-building to the stabilization of the macroeconomic foundation, structural adjustment, rural development and the protection of natural resources. The overall priorities should be the eradication of poverty, the facilitation of a smooth integration into the world economy through the implementation of sustainable development policies and the stabilization of democratic societies.

In the absence of credible and broadly agreed cooperation frameworks of the kind described above, assistance would essentially be limited to humanitarian aid and the prevention of common security risks.

3. TRANSFORMING THE INTERNATIONAL INSTITUTIONS TO PROVIDE GLOBAL GOVERNANCE

In order to facilitate global governance with respect to the promotion of sustainable economic and social development, existing international institutions will have to be gradually transformed. They still largely reflect power structures and a concept of sovereignty predominant at the time they were established. Their number and scope of activities have increased tremendously since the war, but they lack effective mechanisms to ensure policy coherence. Their internal procedures are generally based on consensus diplomacy and lack efficiency. In the economic and social area, the United Nations and its specialized agencies, as a consequence of the North-South but also East-West confrontation, have lost much of their influence to the Bretton Woods institutions, the GATT and informal coordination mechanisms, such as the G7 dominated by the

North. The result has been a lack of legitimacy in global economic policy-making. In addition, regional organizations have generally been too weak to play a major role in either security or economic matters.

It would be unrealistic to expect radical reforms of existing institutions or the establishment of new major institutions in the near future. However, gradual reforms in terms of a clarification of tasks, more efficient procedures, increased participation of underrepresented actors and interinstitutional coherence may be envisaged even in the short and medium term.

3.1. Strengthening global policy initiation, legitimization and implementation

The functions of initiation, legitimization and implementation of global policies need to be reassessed. Initiation requires a degree of coherent leadership which can either come from a core group of influential players – such as the permanent members of the Security Council, the members of the triad or some future configuration combining influence and a degree of representativeness – or from appointed heads of international institutions representing a commonality of interests. Such kinds of leadership are not only necessary to launch new global policy initiatives but also to overcome blockages in multilateral negotiations. To this effect, the functions of heads of international institutions and in particular that of the Secretary-General of the United Nations should be strengthened.

Policy initiation is helped by sound and internationally recognized scientific analysis and by policy advice from independent and highly credible experts. To this effect, on the one hand, the analytical capacities of international institutions need to be strengthened. On the other hand, the establishment of a world council of wise men and women (also representing the interests of future generations) could be envisaged.

116

In the spirit of the universal principle of participatory democracy, an adequate and representative number of governmental and also non-governmental actors (NGOs, representative organizations of social partners) should be involved in a transparent global policy dialogue. However, in order to combine efficiency and legitimacy, it will be necessary to resort more often to a representation of regional or substantial interests through delegation, reconsider traditional consensus procedures for decision-making and rely on instruments of soft law.

The execution and implementation of global policies should be carried out at the appropriate level in accordance with the principle of subsidiarity. The international institutions should focus on ensuring transparency and providing positive incentives for implementation at the local level. They should upgrade monitoring and collective review procedures applying to countries from the South and the North (such as the new GATT trade policy review mechanism). Moreover, credible third-party dispute-settlement procedures on the basis of the rule of law are necessary. In particular, the jurisdiction of the International Court of Justice should be extended.

3.2. Ensuring global policy coherence

The international system consists of a multitude of subsystems with different constituencies (e.g. foreign, defence, finance, trade, development cooperation, environment ministries) and different power and decision-making structures. They operate largely in an uncoordinated manner. It would be Utopian to envisage a radical reform in terms of the establishment of some kind of world government. Rather, the tasks of the subsystems should be clarified, their institutional basis where necessary upgraded and, above all, the mechanisms of coordination and global policy orientation strengthened.

In the area of trade and investment the establishment of a

multilateral trade organization (MTO) points in the right direction provided the interlinkages with the Bretton Woods institutions and the UN are strengthened. The tasks and the policy orientations of the IMF and the World Bank need to be clarified, their internal functioning made more transparent and coordination both between them and with the GATT/MTO and the UN strengthened. In this context, the convening of a new Bretton Woods conference should be considered.

The greatest challenge is the revitalization of the role of the United Nations in the economic and social areas. There are essentially two options: a redefinition of the mandate, composition and functioning of the Security Council and the establishment of a separate UN structure for global sustainable development policy orientation. The first option would require the adoption of an enlarged concept of security extending to economic, social and environmental risks, a more representative membership as far as permanent members are concerned and an abandoning of absolute veto powers. The second option could consist in a reform and upgrading of Ecosoc (Economic and Social Council) in terms of the establishment of a body which could be named the UN Sustainable Development Council with limited representative membership consisting possibly of some permanent members (e.g. Brazil, China, EC, Egypt, India, Japan, Russia, Nigeria, USA), some rotating members and the heads of relevant international institutions (IBRD, IMF, MTO). This body should meet on a permanent basis to monitor the functioning of the global economic and social system, provide guidance for overall policy orientation, including with respect to the Bretton Woods institutions, and propose and decide actions to deal with crisis situations. The recently agreed establishment of a Sustainable Development Commission could be the nucleus for an upgraded political body of this kind. Failing progress in either direction, the G7 process would have to continue to attempt to fill the global policy orientation vacuum and both deepen its institutional structure and modify its membership to become more representative.

3.3. Promoting regional cooperation and integration

The potential of regional and subregional mechanisms of cooperation, policy coordination and integration for the promotion of peace, stability and mutually beneficial development is increasingly recognized, but insufficiently exploited in many regions. In some regions there is a proliferation of overlapping regional initiatives in terms of mandate and membership, while many existing regional institutions have been inefficient even in terms of the limited purposes for which they were set up. Regional mechanisms can, however, be better attuned to the specific needs and features of proximity reflecting cultural traditions and specific models of society. The Community experience has also shown that regional integration efforts can lead to more ambitious and sophisticated models of managing interdependencies and serve as precursor of wider efforts of international cooperation.

Regionalism and multilateralism are thus in principle complementary and mutually supportive. They should not be seen as alternative or conflicting approaches but need to be adjusted to each other. The international community should therefore encourage more strongly efforts of regional cooperation and integration and strengthen the links between regional organizations and international institutions.

Blueprints for regional institutions cannot be established *in abstracto* in view of the diversity of historical experiences, political driving forces and socioeconomic potentials. However, a major global initiative to review obstacles and potentials for the establishment and strengthening of regional institutions would be an important contribution towards the encouragement of more ambitious initiatives in regions lacking efficient cooperative mechanisms.

119

Notes

1   For example, the 1990, 1991 and 1992 World development reports of the World Bank, the 1991 and 1992 Human development reports of the UNDP, the Development cooperation reports of the OECD Development Assistance Committee (DAC), the 1990 report of the South Commission 'The challenge to the South', the Dutch Government report 'A world of difference – A new framework for development cooperation in the 1990s', the 1992 communication of the Commission 'Development cooperation policy in the run-up to 2000', the 1992 report of the Committee on Development and Cooperation of the European Parliament on the new global partnership by Henri Saby.

2   World Commission on Environment and Development, *Our common future*, Oxford University Press, 1987, p. 8.

3   Human development report, 1992, p. 2.

Chapter V

A strategy for the European Community and its Member States

This chapter attempts to identify strategic priorities and policy orientations for the European Community in the light of the analysis of Chapters I to III and the orientations for a global strategy proposed in Chapter IV. In this context, existing Community policies as well as the provisions of the Treaty on European Union are taken as given rather than being analysed in any detail. Finally, the question of necessary changes in the value system of European society is addressed and suggestions are made to increase public awareness and involve European citizens in bringing about these changes.

1. THE PARAMETERS OF A GEOPOLITICAL STRATEGY FOR THE COMMUNITY

The adoption and implementation of the global strategy proposed in the previous chapter going far beyond traditional multilateral action would require strong efforts of conviction, both within the Community and in relation to its international partners. As has been argued in Chapter I, the Community and its Member States should have a strong geopolitical interest in contributing to the design of such a strategy. In considering this option, the specific nature of the Community – its possibilities and limitations – must be taken into account.

The Community, while having a growing weight in the international system, has never clearly defined its basic geopolitical interests and priorities, due to disagreement among Member States and inadequate institutional support. Moreover, the Community has had (and still has) only a reduced scope of action, as well as limited competencies and means to intervene in global affairs. The Member States of the Community, on the other hand, in particular the large ones, have acted as full participants in international affairs on the basis of their own geopolitical interests and means, while their capacity as individual countries to influence the international system has been on the decline.

The discrepancy between the potential and reality of European influence in world affairs was of secondary importance as long as the East-West conflict predominated. The changing nature of the international system and of the external challenges which the Community and its Member States face, however, force the Community to clarify its external identity and priorities. It also offers new options for doing so in a manner which reflects its hybrid nature.

As described in the first chapter, the emerging poles of the post-Yalta system interact in a different manner compared to the cold war period. Economic forces and threats of a non-military nature gain in importance while local conflicts spread. Hegemonic relations between States are no longer a viable basis for dealing effectively with global challenges and security risks. Even powerful countries, including the USA, can no longer meet challenges everywhere on the planet and are increasingly forced to cooperate in coalitions and at the multilateral level. The nature of the new challenges calls for a global agreement between international actors on an enlarged concept of cooperative security, more effective mechanisms of cooperative management of interdependencies and a more reasonable sharing of power and burdens. In short, it is a manifestation of soft power that is likely to characterize increasingly the international system.

The European Community should be in a good position to contribute to the design of a viable multilateral strategy in the new geopolitical context. It is itself the expression of soft power, not only because of the *acquis communitaire*, but also because of the wider system of cooperation among Member States. It is also gradually moving from an international organization *sui generis*, in which consensus is primarily based on a brokerage of national interests, towards a political entity, in which consensus is based on the perception of a common interest. However, this political entity cannot be based on a unitarian model. It must respect the continued existence of national identities and interests and reflect this in its internal division of powers and tasks.

The previous chapters have demonstrated that North-South relations can no longer be based primarily upon (bilateral) development cooperation between northern donors and southern recipients, but require more permanent and systemic multilateral policies in the economic, social, humanitarian, ecological and demographic domains. The participation of all major actors is a precondition to formulate and implement such policies. In view of its internal experience, the Community would seem particularly well equipped to initiate such policies. Moreover, no single actor has the means to assemble the critical mass of resources to deal with structural problems adequately everywhere in the world. The establishment of geographical priorities, based on fundamental interests and means, is therefore inevitable, including for the Community taking into account the necessity of an effective internal division of tasks.

These basic considerations on the profoundly changing international system, both outside and within Europe, provide

123

the parameters for the establishment of geopolitical priorities allowing the Community to assert itself as an international actor in promoting sustainable social and economic development, as agreed in the Maastricht Treaty. They should also help to provide the basic criteria for a division of competences and tasks between the Community and its Member States. In the past, this division of competences and tasks has not been based on a coherent philosophy and a long-term view on the role of the Community in the world. The geopolitical priorities of the Community may best be defined in relation to the major challenges and risks that affect the global system as well as those affecting the Community, more specifically. This has geographical and systemic implications for the means and levels of intervention of the Community, since sustainable social and economic development is primarily hindered by structural shortcomings occurring at the global, regional and local levels.

2. EXTERNAL POLICY ORIENTATIONS

Relations between the Community *sensu stricto* and the developing countries have been largely the result of post-colonial history and specific ties between some Member States and their former colonies. They have been gradually extended and diversified in response to external and internal pressures in particular from new Member States wanting to see their geographical priorities better reflected. Their rooting in paternalistic interests has resulted in a somewhat arbitrary and inflexible *acquis*. This has had two consequences.

First, the present Community policies towards the developing world do not seem to be based on a real consensus within the Community on priorities and means. They tend to be the result of political brokering between Member States lacking a comprehensive common vision. Consequently, they are often short of addressing identified challenges in accordance with the

Community's interests and in a coherent manner. This has frustrated, to a certain extent, the degree of commitment to these policies in some Member States.

Second, a range of specific instruments and financial appropriations have been created, mostly as a result of short-term political compromises rather than of a far-reaching and coherent Community strategy. These instruments also do not always reflect a demonstrable added value *vis-à-vis* the development cooperation policies of individual Member States.

The pursuit of the overall goal of promoting a coherent framework for North-South relations and sustainable social and economic development does not require that the Community substitutes itself for its Member States in this area. The Community should, on the other hand, be much more than simply a 13th donor. It should pursue policies that clearly bear a value-added element and are not perceived as competing with the cooperation policies of its Member States. Furthermore, too wide a geographical and instrumental spread of means weakens the ability of the Community to set priorities and respond to systemic challenges and risks related to geographical proximity.

What then and where is the added value of the Community in implementing a geopolitical and geoeconomic strategy? How can an adequate division of tasks between the Community and its Member States be defined with a view to strengthening the Community in such a way that it is better able to use its advantages as a soft power in promoting sustainable social and economic development globally? The answers to these questions should be based on efficiency and coherence.

In the light of the above-mentioned observations, the Community's priorities should be twofold, namely multilateral strategies to deal with systemic issues and regional strategies concerning its geographical proximity.

2.1. Multilateral and systemic priorities: managing global interdependencies

With regard to the management of economic globalization, the Community, building on its role in GATT, should aim to become a full participant in all multilateral organizations that govern international trade, financial and monetary relations. This would allow the Community to use its full potential and weight as a soft power in order to reinforce the coherence of international economic relations, which is essential to the promotion of sustainable social and economic development. As a matter of priority, and also as a logical and necessary consequence of the eventual implementation of the European monetary union, the Community should become a full member of such institutions as the future Multilateral Trade Organization, the International Monetary Fund, the World Bank and the Bank for International Settlements and speak with one voice.

The Community should also extend its participation in the G7 and use this forum to initiate new policies and institutional reforms as outlined in Chapter IV. However, in the longer term, its aim should be to make this type of intergovernmental arrangement limited to a few northern countries obsolete, by bringing the issues at stake with regard to global governance back to the proper multilateral institutions where they belong. Indeed, the Community should promote deep integration at the global level, both as a condition for sustainable development and as a consequence of the implementation of international good governance. This requires close cooperation within the triad, which inevitably will have to assume a leadership role. However, the twin risks of economic marginalization and free-riders call for a multilateralization of deep integration strategies.

The other global priorities, such as peace and security, democracy, protection of human rights, demography, environment, migration, poverty, pandemics and drugs, equally require concerted international action and call for Community leadership and participation as such in the relevant multilateral institutions. In these areas, the added value and strength of the Community would seem to lie primarily in policy definition and initiation, negotiation, coordination and rule-making, while implementation could be essentially left to Member States. Of particular importance in this context will be the reinforcement and extension of the political and economic dialogue of the Community and its Member States with regions of developing countries (e.g. Rio Group, ASEAN, San José Group, Gulf Cooperation Council).

More generally, the Community should concentrate its efforts on the promotion of horizontal and systemic policies to deal more effectively with structural shortcomings occurring at the global, regional and local levels. It would need to increase its budgetary means for common actions in support of such policies. However, taking into account the know-how and specific priorities of Member States and the proposition that the Community should not act as a 13th Member State in development cooperation, the Community may well limit its involvement in geographically defined development cooperation policies essentially to questions of orientation, coordination and negotiation of policy frameworks, such as the development contracts described in Chapter IV. It could also devolve the implementation of common actions to domestic or, where appropriate, multilateral agencies.

Specific common actions related to systemic challenges (as well as development cooperation programmes of multilateral agencies and EC Member States) would thus be continued and extended in the different regions (sub-Saharan Africa, Latin America, Asia). In budgetary terms, this could mean a progressive transfer of funds from the current regional apportionment of development cooperation budget lines to systemic and horizontal budget lines. These systemic budget lines should be substantially extended *inter alia* to cover multilateral organizations and facilities (e.g. the World Bank's Global Environment Facility). Equally, their endowments should be considerably increased. Moreover, the external activities of the European Investment Bank should be progressively reoriented towards the financing of systemic objectives. An additional advantage of the proposal to define more clearly the Community's geopolitical priorities would thus be more coherence of the Community's financial framework with regard to external actions.

Since sub-Saharan Africa is particularly afflicted by structural problems and systemic challenges, the international community, both multilateral and bilateral donors, will have to assume a special and increased responsibility in political and financial terms towards this region, with a strong emphasis on 'development contracts' as described in Chapter IV. The multilateral engagement for Africa will have to be of a larger magnitude than in other regions, encompassing the Community and its Member States, the USA, Japan and other OECD Member States, as well as Latin American and Asian States and, of course, the international financial institutions. The fundamental objective of a multilateral strategy should be to generate and implement structural solutions for Africa's profound problems. An important element of such a strategy could be a regional system of payments anchored on a multilateral monetary facility. The successful implementation of such a mechanism will also depend on the reform of the Bretton Woods institutions as outlined in Chapter IV, in which the Community should play a major role.

The Community could assume a leading role both in promoting such a multilateral approach and in ensuring a smooth transition from the Lomé scheme to the implementation of multilateral development contracts. Together with the World Bank, it could take the lead in coordinating development contracts with African countries. The budgetization of the European Development Fund would help to reorient the

Community's policy towards sub-Saharan Africa and make it more accountable. The next revision of the European Development Fund to be completed in 1995 could be an appropriate occasion to consider such a reorientation.

Community and Member States' action in the area of development cooperation would thus over time become internally more coherent, be integrated in a multilateral framework with all major agencies and individual donors, including NGOs, and be enshrined in development contracts as described in Chapter IV. An important element in this context would be the establishment of clear Community rules on untied aid, as a fundamental step towards the establishment of binding rules on such aid at the multilateral level. This could also serve to strengthen South/South and South/East commercial flows.

2.2. Regional responsibilities: managing geographical proximity

The Community's second main interest is to promote peace, stability and development in its direct neighbourhood. The end of the East-West conflict and the declining involvement of the USA in Europe's security, drive the Community to define itself in terms of a political entity and assume an increasing role in filling the emerging power vacuum in its wider region.

Moreover, the long-term developments in the Community's direct proximity contain uncertainties that could affect its internal cohesion and capacity to act. Its interests and responsibilities go beyond those of individual Member States. This means that the Community should give the highest priority to the promotion of sustainable social and economic development in these regions. The instruments that are needed to reach these goals will have to be adjusted to the specific requirements of the different regions. In these regions, the Member States will, of course, continue to be

129

active individually. However, to be efficient, their policies should be subject to an overall and coherent Community framework.

A coherent policy approach towards Central, Eastern and South-Eastern Europe and the non-Community countries of the Mediterranean region, including Turkey and the Middle East, will have to respond to the challenges of demography, environment, and economic and political instability. It would seek to promote peaceful integration within and between these regions. The establishment of regional security regimes (such as the Conference on Security and Cooperation in Europe (CSCE) and a CSCE for the Mediterranean) should be an integral part of a comprehensive European doctrine of geographical proximity.

Vis-à-vis the countries of Central, Eastern and South-Eastern Europe, the policy priorities set out in the Commission's reports to the Lisbon and Edinburgh Summits (deepening of political dialogue, strengthening of Europe Agreements, creation of a wider European free trade area) and the orientations agreed by the Copenhagen Summit concerning, in particular, the conditions for membership could be complemented by the establishment of pan-European infrastructural networks and the promotion of cross-border region-to-region and town-to-town cooperation, including in the relations between these countries. Further deep integration should be fostered to facilitate the progressive implementation of the four freedoms and eventually full membership. In addition, initiatives towards a pan-European security order need to be vigorously pursued.

With regard to the non-Community southern Mediterranean countries, including Turkey, the Maghreb and the Mashrek countries, the Community should aim to create an economic cooperation zone based on the recent Commission proposals on cooperation with the Maghreb countries, progressively leading to a free trade area with the Community. This would require substantial financial and technological transfers in order to lay the foundations of internal cohesion and sustainability in the region. The overall objectives of this approach would be to alleviate political, security, demographic, migratory and environmental pressures.

The establishment of free trade areas, customs unions and other types of regional cooperation zones among the countries of Central, Eastern and South-Eastern Europe (as crucial phases on their way towards full EC membership), on the one hand, and among CIS and non-Community Mediterranean countries, on the other hand, would constitute building blocks towards their integration into the economy of the Community. For these regions, a regional system of payments linked to the Community, as a support for intraregional trade, could be considered. Moreover, the existing budgetary lines and financial protocols destined for these countries could be gradually replaced by structural funds, an approach which is more in line with the Community's cohesion policies than with traditional development cooperation strategies. Access to these structural funds could be applied in a manner similar to the current rules governing the intra-Community Structural Funds (cofinancing). Concerning private investments, which are to a large extent hindered because of political risks, a Community-wide risk reinsurance system concerning certain legal changes should be considered.

3. INTERNAL POLICY COHERENCE

Divergences between policies of Member States and inconsistencies of Community policies often lead to contradictory signals with regard to the goals of sustainability and produce negative repercussions both inside and outside the Community. Too often these policies are dictated by short-term views that do not take into account the environmental and social dimensions of economic growth.

First, divergences in macroeconomic policies, such as

different monetary and fiscal policies, hinder economic growth both inside and outside the Community. Industrial, R&D, consumer, energy and environment policies are inadequately adjusted to the objective of promoting the sustainability of economic and social development both in the EC and beyond. Some Community policies, in particular the common agricultural policy (CAP), are widely believed to have been fundamentally in contradiction with this objective.

Second, the access to the Community markets for agricultural and industrial products from developing countries is a key part of any structural policy promoting sustainable social and economic development. This means that further and deeper reforms of the CAP and commercial policies will be unavoidable in order to reduce trade restrictions and distortions. However, in order to avoid serious political, social and economic problems in the Community, such reforms will have to be implemented in parallel with credible adjustment policies. In particular, targeted policies, including incentives for investments in environmentally friendly sectors, aiming to restructure economic activities in exposed zones will have to be devised. This calls for appropriate industrial, R&D, agricultural, fiscal (ecotaxes as well as tax exemptions), environmental and consumer policies in terms of stimulating renovation and modernization of new economic opportunities, as well as temporary adjustment of sunset sectors.

The further opening of Community markets to developing countries' exports also provides additional leverage to encourage the environmental and social dimensions of economic growth in the South in terms of adequate commitments of developing countries in the framework of development contracts, for example by linking the granting of specific advantages to special efforts in these areas. From the side of the Community, substantial transfers of appropriate technology, as well as the means to diffuse it, will be required.

In order to promote the goal of sustainable social and

economic development, the following measures could be considered by the Commission:

(i) a general review of how the various Community policies affect development in the South;
(ii) the establishment of procedures for the assessment of the impact of major new policy proposals by the Commission on the goals of social and economic sustainable development and, in particular, their consequences for developing countries.

The financing of the required common actions and strategies aiming to provide the South, in particular Africa, with better development perspectives cannot be implemented without additional resources which could come from energy taxes, coordinated Community efforts to reach the 0.7% of GDP ODA objective, reduction of military expenditure, a Community 'solidarity' loan and a reallocation of financial means including import duties. Moreover, additional resources can be generated through the reforms of the international monetary and financial system described in Chapter IV, as well as the implementation of the economic and monetary union.

4. EUROPEAN SOCIETY AND THE WORLD'S LONG-TERM CHALLENGES

The implementation of the geopolitical strategy proposed for the Community – while improving conditions for sustainable social and economic development in the short to medium term and providing a politically realistic margin of flexibility – does not sufficiently address the seriousness of the long-term global interdependencies and risks analysed in Chapter III.

Nothing less than a reorientation of production and consumption habits and patterns and the underlying social values will be sufficient in the longer term. In other words, the basic aim is to encourage a development of industrial societies that is compatible with sustainable social and economic development.

Changes in societal values usually emerge as a result of pressures from civil society in interaction with political authorities, and not from unilateral imposition of measures by those authorities. Because of the complexity of such interaction, the room for manoeuvre and the power of public authorities at local, regional, national or Community level to impose changes from above are limited. Also, the necessary comprehensive legislation at Community level can at best be adopted over time.

Therefore, the short- and medium-term strategies proposed above would have to be accompanied by actions of public authorities that aim to stimulate and support existing and emerging trends in civil society, pave the way to sustainable social and economic development and permit the progressive introduction of comprehensive legislation. Public action should gather support for a reorientation of consumption and production patterns by contributing to the development of public awareness of the risks of an unlimited continuation of present global trends.

The nature of these global trends is such that, without profound changes in northern patterns of consumption and production and a deeper understanding of the complexity of North-South interdependencies, authoritarian measures by political authorities could become unavoidable in case of acute aggravation of political, environmental and demographic incidents and pressures. A deeper awareness of the nature of these global trends could also contribute to the prevention of the emergence or strengthening of extremist and irrational ideologies which constitute a threat to democracy.

The following initiatives by public authorities could contribute to strengthening the awareness of civil society with regard to the necessary reorientation of the Western model of society:

(i) The encouragement of an active involvement of national, European and international non-governmental organizations in the social and, especially, political debate, and their formal and regular participation in the different stages of the decision-making process on issues relating to sustainable development. In this respect, consultation procedures, such as public parliamentary hearings, could be considerably developed within the Community. At the international level, the Community could support an active participation of NGOs in international forums and bodies, such as the Sustainable Development Commission, the World Population Summit in 1994 or the World Social Summit to be held in 1995.

(ii) Community-wide planning to prepare for the adoption and implementation of long-term strategies in favour of alternative development patterns at times when risk awareness in the public is high (e.g. in the aftermath of an ecological or development disaster).

(iii) The formation of a voluntary Community service in which qualified young citizens of all Member States could serve together in developing countries that have concluded development contracts with the community of donors. If this were done on a reasonably large scale, Europeans would not only get a better understanding of North-South interdependencies, but also strengthen their awareness of the need to change Western patterns of production and consumption.

(iv) The establishment of European media and educational programmes to raise public awareness of global interdependencies and risks.

(v) The establishment of a code of conduct for EC companies, including subsidiaries of foreign companies in the EC and subsidiaries of EC companies in foreign countries, to encourage promotion of sustainable social and economic development.

(vi) The floating on the European financial markets of a Community-wide solidarity loan. It would aim to finance projects and programmes in developing countries aiming to replace natural capital stock. The shareholders in this solidarity loan could benefit from a guaranteed minimum return and fiscal advantages, including a reduction of succession duties. This would emphasize the intergenerational solidarity that this loan would seek to provide.

(vii) Twinning between EC and southern cities supported by substantive cooperation funds.

These few practical suggestions on strengthening the awareness of Europes citizens of the need to fundamentally change the Western way of life do not constitute sufficient ground for a comprehensive strategy. Much more is needed. The shift towards new patterns of consumption and production will be greatly aided particularly if new technological choices and economic analysis tools become available.

(i) Strong action, supported by adequate financial means, needs be taken in order to direct basic and applied technological research towards social and economic sustainability. This means not only supporting the existing lines of research on new environmentally friendly materials and reduction of energy consumption for physical output, but further reinforcing the current trend towards a post-industrial society based on more immaterial patterns of production and consumption, as well as anthropocentric systems of production with an emphasis on human skills and training as a means of curbing overcapitalization. On the same line, a more collective energy-saving-pattern of consumption for physical goods should be promoted (e.g. collective transport).

136

(ii) The Community should build on its geographical, cultural and climatic diversity to develop environmentally appropriate technologies that are suitable to be transferred and diffused in developing countries, thus strengthening their sustainable economic and social development, particularly in the field of urban planning, energy, transport, agriculture and protection of natural capital stock.

(iii) Last, but not least, in order to promote successfully sustainable economic and social development on a global world scale, it is imperative for policy-making and for convincing public opinion to develop specific tools which would adequately measure the relationship between the environment and the economy, as well as the social consequences of economic activities. In this context, efforts should be made to integrate the environmental and social costs of economic activities in the national accounting systems. Moreover, analytical tools will have to be developed to ameliorate the understanding of physical processes of environmental degradation.

Annex 1

The evolution of North–South relations and development thinking since the war

1. 1945–60: THE CONSTRUCTION OF A LIBERAL UNIVERSAL SYSTEM AND THE EMERGENCE OF THE SOUTH[1]

The institutional and conceptual framework for North–South relations has conditioned the experiences of countries since the political and legal foundations were laid at the end of World War II. Institutionally, three events stand out: the Bretton Woods Conference of 1944 establishing the International Bank for Reconstruction and Development (World Bank) and the International Monetary Fund (IMF), the San Francisco Conference of 1945 establishing the United Nations and the General Agreement on Tariffs and Trade (GATT) which entered into force (provisionally) in 1947. Conceptually, these institutions were based on liberal thinking, namely the recognition of the equality of sovereign States and the promotion of peace and security, human rights and economic freedoms. Politically, they were a response both to the experience of the war and to the breakdown of the monetary, financial and trading order in the 1930s.

Procedurally, the exercise of influence within these organizations was conditioned in different manners affecting their operational capacities and evolution. The simple majority rule on the basis of one country/one vote allowed developing countries, whose numbers were increasing as decolonization progressed, to impose their views in the context of nonbinding resolutions adopted by the United Nations General Assembly. The same was not possible in the Security Council because of the veto powers of its five permanent members. The influence of developing countries remained marginal in the Bretton Woods institutions where voting rights are based on capital shares and the GATT where the major trading partners dominate the negotiations and decisions taken by consensus.

The Allied powers thus fenced the southern States, of which there were few outside Latin America at the time, into a system of their construction. In response, the independent southern States emerging in the era of decolonization tried to adopt common positions under the aegis of the Non-Aligned Movement.[2] Their initial approach was to focus on political sovereignty and independence with little perception of divergent economic interests between the technologically advanced North constructing its war-hit economies and their economically dependent South. The prevailing mood of the period was that poor countries should copy the model of northern industrial society by rapidly constructing an industrial base – rivalry existing over the choices between and within the capitalist and Marxist paths.

2. 1960–73: BETWEEN IMITATION AND AUTONOMY

During the 1960s, North–South agreements and institution-building at the bilateral, regional and multilateral levels followed decolonization as the ex-colonies were tied into the evolving global framework.[3] The philosophy of benevolent assistance and cooperation pervaded these agreements with the problem of development perceived as overcoming obstacles to the full realization of these countries' economic capacities. However, as early as 1969 the UN-commissioned Pearson report concluded that development assistance was in a crisis due to its orientation towards the short-term political, strategic and export interests of donor countries. The 1970 General Assembly Resolution 2676 committing developed countries to allocate 0.7% of GDP for official development assistance (ODA) contained no deadline and has only been respected by the Scandinavian countries and the Netherlands.

In this period, the newly independent developing countries were still defining their position in a bipolar world. Those closer to the Western bloc favoured the development strategies offered by writers such as Rostow who thought imitating earlier Western policies could foster a 'take-off' in their societies' productive capacities.[4] In gearing the economy to industrial growth, the spread of welfare was believed to come from the trickle-down effect.[5]

Those in the ambit of the Eastern bloc adopted Marxist-Leninist centralized planning models inspired by Soviet and, to a lesser extent, Chinese experiences in which the State controlled by a single party dictated all economic decisions.

The meagre results of modernization policies and external assistance prompted Third World intellectuals and political leaders to question the relationship of developing countries to the world economy. Raul Prebisch and the Economic Commission for Latin America's work in the 1950s influenced government policy especially in Latin America towards the adoption of strategies of import substitution industrialization. The rationale for their strategy was that given the deteriorating terms of trade for primary products against manufactured goods, a long-term transfer of income would only occur if indigenous industry was developed behind tariff and quantitative trade barriers. More radical alternative development theories, under the heading of 'dependencia', explained underdevelopment as a consequence of dependence on industrialized countries rather than inadequate integration into the international economy and pleaded either in favour of autonomous socialist development strategies or at least self-reliance.

In all these strategies and theories, the development of the agricultural sector, human resources and adequate institutions were widely neglected. Indeed, the agricultural sector was often discriminated against, in both policy and development thought.[6]

3. 1973–82: BETWEEN ECONOMIC CRISIS AND THE SEARCH FOR A NEW INTERNATIONAL ECONOMIC ORDER

The beginning of the 1970s was economically marked by the collapse of the Bretton Woods exchange-rate system and the first oil crisis. The mounting monetary instability, the fall in the value of the US dollar, in which most raw materials were priced, and the sharp rise in oil prices led to rising revenues of OPEC countries but low if not negative per capita growth rates for poor oil-importing developing countries. Some newly industrializing countries (NICs), especially in East Asia, continued to enjoy economic growth. Their success lay in the encouragement given through the interplay between the State and business to their maturing industries to produce goods for export, their governments support for the agricultural sector and their commitment to education and training. In contrast, agriculture and education were neglected, particularly in Africa, and the industries of Latin America and Africa faltered in their attempts to replace imported goods behind government-imposed trade barriers. The result was a growing diversity of development patterns in southern hemisphere countries.

The example of the oil-price cartel, the easy availability of financial resources and ideas of structural imbalance in world trade, lent weight to the demand for a new international economic order (NIEO). The request for the NIEO was in terms of an action programme and a Charter of Economic Rights and Duties of States adopted at the sixth special session of the UN General Assembly, after formulation by the Non-Aligned Movement in Algiers in 1973. In particular, the action programme called for global negotiations on altering the structural imbalance of the world economy.[7] Responses from industrialized countries, who were generally opposed for ideological and economic reasons, were either low key (the USA digesting the Vietnam war) or paternalistic (the Community concluding the first Lomé agreement). Responses from multinational organizations reflected this new thinking, with the World Bank promoting a 'redistribution with growth' approach (under McNamara) and the ILO a 'basic needs' strategy. Both approaches criticized the traditional growth strategies in the light of persisting inequalities and rising poverty, favouring instead more Keynesian policies.

The global North-South negotiations nevertheless remained largely a dialogue of the deaf. Developing countries turned – at least conceptually – to the idea of South/South cooperation and collective self-reliance (Arusha 1979) as the second oil-price shock further weakened their economics. However, the internal causes of underdevelopment (overemphasis on industrialization through import substitution, exclusion of large parts of the population, inadequate government structures) were still not seriously addressed in most countries. Neither the first report of the Brandt Commission of 1980 entitled 'North-South: A programme for survival' nor the 1981 North-South Summit in Cancun calling for a massive transfer of resources managed to revive the North-South dialogue in view of the slowdown in world growth, rising Third World debts and a neo-conservative supply-side deregulation ideology in the North which also influenced the direction of the Bretton Woods institutions in the 1980s.

143

4. 1982–91: FROM THE DEBT CRISIS TO THE END OF THE EAST-WEST CONFLICT

Mexico's inability to meet its debt obligations and its subsequent suspension of debt servicing in August 1982 triggered off an international financial crisis. Rising debt resulted from the hidden costs of import substitution policies (after the initial 'easy' stage), lenient lending, a sharp rise in interest rates, a deterioration of the terms of trade and trade protectionism. In particular, Latin American and African economies were strongly affected by the sudden decline of financial transfers having overexposed their economies. As a consequence, from this period to the present day, these regions have suffered from net financial transfers to the lending countries and international institutions despite various plans for debt rescheduling or reconversion (Baker 1985, Brady 1989).

The debt crisis provoked a reorientation of development cooperation and internal policies in the name of structural adjustment. These policies represented a watershed in development cooperation. They moved away from conditioning assistance largely on the grounds of political allegiance. Under the leadership of the IMF and the World Bank, financial assistance was now conditioned on radical reforms of internal economic policies within developing countries with the emphasis on more realistic exchange rates, balanced budgets, freeing of domestic prices, export promotion and opening-up of internal markets to international competition. The adjustment policies were designed to strengthen the competitiveness of the affected economies. However, at least in the short term, they tended to lead to very low and, in many cases, negative growth rates, a deterioration of living conditions for the poorest population groups and environmental degradation. The social fraction and societal transformation produced by these policies

144

were heavily criticized and not just by the 'dependencia' theorists.[8] As a consequence, in recent years more attention has been given to the alleviation of the social costs of structural adjustments.[9] Within the ascendant liberal-capitalist paradigm, the realization that poverty was taking a structural nature in some countries provoked a shift of emphasis onto family planning, educational and infrastructural deficits and strategies to overcome the persistence of dual economies and marginalization.[10]

The 1980s are widely considered to have been a 'lost decade' in terms of development for the majority of southern hemisphere countries even though some regions continued to experience fast growth rates and despite the 'new realist' arguments that the decade had been characterized by a necessary learning process. In any event, the result was a further increase in the heterogeneity of the 'South', raising questions about the continued justification of this notion. The trend to further marginalization of many developing countries was reinforced while the international system has come to be increasingly dominated by the triad of economic powers – Europe, Japan and the USA. The North-South dialogue was dead and the focus of international attention drifted further away from the UN bodies to the Bretton Woods institutions, the GATT (embarking on the Uruguay Round multilateral trade negotiations) and the G7 economic summits.

The decline and fall of the Soviet imperium at the turn of the decade were widely perceived as opening a new window of opportunity for North-South relations as developing countries would no longer be the victims of hegemonic struggles over spheres of influence. It also led to an increasing acceptance of the values of democratic government and market-friendly economic policies, so long pushed by the West. This has mixed with a perception of exponential population growth, environmental threats and structural poverty to produce a new awareness of international inter-

145

dependences and shared responsibilities. This new awareness has, in particular, been promoted by the 1989 report of the Brundtland Commission 'Our common future' which led to the United Nations Conference on Environment and Development in June 1992 in Rio. However, as the international economy staggers and the industrialized countries shift their focus to the transformation process in the East, developing countries are becoming increasingly worried that development assistance may be diverted and their market access affected by the integration of the East into world markets.

Notes

1   The presentation draws on Comeliau, C. *Les relations Nord-Sud*, éditions La découverte, 1991, as well as the Dutch Government report 'A world of difference – A new framework for development cooperation in the 1990s', The Hague, 1991. The observations on development thinking are inspired by Oman, C. and Wignaraja, G. 'The post-war evolution of development thinking', OECD Development Centre, 1991.
2   As a political notion, the 'South' came into being at the Bandung Conference of 1955 as a consequence of a shared philosophy of anti-colonialism and non-alignment.
3   For example, the Yaounde Association Agreement between the European Community and 18 African ex-colonies, Kennedys alliance for progress with Latin America, the creation of the Development Assistance Committee of the OECD and the establishment of Unctad.
4   Rostow, W.W. 'The stages of economic growth: A non-communist manifesto', 1960.
5   See, in particular, Leibenstein, H. 'Investment criteria, productivity and economic development', 1955.
6   See, for example, Lewis. W. A. 'Economic development with unlimited supplies of labour', 1954.
7   The action programme promoted concepts such as economic sovereignty, trade liberalization and structural adjustment of

developing countries, increased technology transfer and control of multinational companies, stabilization of commodity prices at higher levels (integrated commodity programme and common fund), reforms of the monetary system towards more stable exchange rates and better credit facilities, increases in ODA, debt rescheduling and better developing country representation in the international economic organizations.

8 See, for example, Dornbush, R. 'Stabilization in developing countries: What have we learned?' *World Development*, Vol. 10, No. 9 1982; Fishlow, A. 'El estado de la ciencia económica en América Latina' in *Progreso Económico y Social en América Latina*, 1985.

9 See Unicef study 'Adjustment with a human face' (eds. G. A. Gomia, R. Jolly, F. Steward), 1987; World Bank report 'Social dimensions of adjustments', 1987; World Bank report 'Sub-Saharan Africa – from crisis to sustainable growth: A long-term prospective study', 1989.

10 See, for example, the chairman's report of the OECD Development Assistance Committee, 'Twenty-five years of development cooperation', 1985.

Annex 2

BALANCE SHEET OF HUMAN DEVELOPMENT – DEVELOPING COUNTRIES[1]

Progress	Deprivation
Average life expectancy is now 63 years – 17 years more than in 1960.	14 million children die every year before they reach the age of five.
Two thirds of people have ready access to health services.	Nearly 1.5 billion people still lack access to health services.
Access to safe water has increased in the past 20 years by more than two thirds.	1.3 billion people still lack access to safe water.
Public expenditure on health as a proportion of GNP increased by nearly 50% in the past 30 years.	2.3 billion people lack access to sanitation.
Daily calorie supply is now about 110% of the overall requirement (compared with 90% some 25 years ago).	More than a quarter of the world's people do not get enough food, and nearly one billion go hungry. Over 100 million people were affected by famine in 1990.
The adult literacy rate has increased by more than one third since 1970.	Over 300 million children do not attend primary or secondary school.
Nearly three quarters of children are enrolled in school.	Nearly one billion adults are illiterate, nearly 600 million of them women.

More than 2% of GDP is spent on social security benefits.	1.2 billion still barely survive in absolute poverty.
Employee earnings grew some 3% annually in the 1980s, twice the rate in the 1970s and more than that in industrial countries.	About half the people in sub-Saharan Africa are below the poverty line.
The mortality rate of young children has been halved in the last 30 years.	Infant mortality figures in the poorest nations are 115 per 1,000 live births. Nearly one million children in sub-Saharan Africa are infected with HIV.
The immunization rate for one-year-old children has increased from one quarter to more than three quarters during the past 10 years.	180 million young children are still malnourished.
The male-female gaps in primary education have decreased by a half in the past 20 to 30 years, and in literacy by one third in the past 20 years.	Women receive on average only half the higher education of men. Female representation in parliament is only 14% that of males.

[1] *Source*: UNDP Human development report, 1992, p. 14.

Annex 3

'NORTH-SOUTH FORWARD STUDIES' – STUDY BRIEF GIVEN TO THE FORWARD STUDIES UNIT

The increasing inequality between the situations of the rich and poor countries of the world is a threat to balanced North–South relations, and in the years to come it will be exacerbated by population growth and deterioration of the environment. The importance of the changes which have occurred in Eastern Europe must not be allowed to obscure these global trends which, over the next 10 to 20 years, are certain to transform relations between northern and southern countries.

Against this background, the Forward Studies Unit is requested to submit a report by June 1992 setting out an analysis and strategic guidelines.

Firstly, a forward description must be made of the new shape of relations between North and South with particular reference to the diversification of the southern countries, the emergence of the East European countries and the main aspects of world interdependence, which, apart from the basic 'currency-trade-finance' triangle, must henceforth include the environment, population growth and greater population mobility. This description must be followed by guidelines for improving the world institutional system in the light of a shared North–South objective of 'sustainable development'.

Secondly, on this basis, the Unit must define geopolitical priorities for the European Community and guidelines for achieving them. The Community will be perceived as an 'active contributor', either as an active participant in the definition of rules of the multilateral system compatible with its interests, or as a partner in international cooperation or, lastly, as an initiator of internal policies with major external implications.

The report must suggest practical ways of interesting the European public in these long-term objectives. The Unit must work in close collaboration with the Directorates-General concerned, which will be invited to take part in the meetings of an open working party to gather the ideas of experts or external witnesses. No recourse will be made to consultants.

Selected bibliography

Alexandratos, N. '1988 world agriculture: Towards 2000', an FAO study.

Bertelsmann Foundation. *Challenges in the Mediterranean – The European response*, 1991.

Brown, M. and Goldin, I. *The future of agriculture: Developing country implications*, OECD Development Centre, 1990.

Bustelo Gómez, P. 'Economía política de los nuevos países industriales asiáticos', *Siglo Veintiuno de España*, Madrid, 1990.

Centre d'études prospectives et d'informations internationales. *Économie mondiale 1990–2000: L'impératif de croissance*, 1992.

Chesnais, J.-C. and Seibel, C. *L'évolution sociodémographique: Éléments prospectifs*.

Cohen-Tanugi, L. *L'Europe en danger*, Paris, 1992.

Comeliau, C. *Les relations Nord-Sud*, éditions La découverte, 1991.

Davenport, M. and Page, S. *Europe 1992 and the developing world*, Overseas Development Institute, 1991.

de Soto, H. *El otro sendero*, Lima, 1986.

Dornbush, R. 'Stabilization in developing countries: What have we learned?' *World Development*, Vol. 10, No 9, 1982.

Dunning, A. B. 'Poverty and the environment: Reversing the downward spiral', *Worldwatch Paper 92*, 1989.

Dutch Government. 'A world of difference – A new framework for development cooperation in the 1990s', report, The Hague, 1991.

Emmerij, L. *La grenade dégoupillée*, Paris, 1992.

European Commission. 'Energy in the future – A view to the future', September 1992.

European Commission. 'Development cooperation in the run-up to 2000', 15 May 1992.

European Commission. 'Population trends and Europe', report, Forward Studies Unit, 1990.

European Parliament. Report on the spread of organized crime linked to drugs trafficking in the Member States of the European Community, 1992.

European Parliament. Report of the Committee on Development and Cooperation on the new global partnership by H. Saby, 1992.

FAO. 'Recent developments in world fisheries', April 1991.

Fishlow, A. 'El estado de la ciencia económica en América Latina', in *Progreso Económico y Social en América Latina*, 1985.

Freedman, L. 'Order and disorder in the new world', *Foreign Affairs*, No 1, 1992.

GATT. *International trade 1989–90*, 1991–92.

George, S. *The debt boomerang*, 1992.

Golding, J. and van der Meersbrugge, D. *Trade liberalization: What's at stake?*, OECD Development Centre policy brief, 1992.

Independent Commission on International Development (Brandt Commission). *North-South: A programme for survival*, 1980.

International Monetary Fund. *World economic outlook*, May 1993.

Jacquemin, A. and Wright, D. *The European challenges post-1992; Shaping factors, shaping actors*, 1993.

Kahler, M. 'The international political economy', *Foreign Affairs*, autumn, 1990.

Krauthammer, C. 'The unipolar moment', in Allison, G. T. and Treverton, G. T. (eds), *Rethinking American security: Beyond cold war to new world order*, New York, Norton, 1992.

Laïdi, Z. (ed.), *L'ordre mondial relâché*, Paris, 1992.

Leibenstein, H. *Investment criteria, productivity and economic development*, 1955.

Lewis, W. A. *Economic development with unlimited supplies of labour*, 1954.

Netherlands Central Planning Bureau. 'Scanning the future. A long-term study of the world economy', report, The Hague, 1992.

OECD. 'Long-term prospectives of the world economy', report, 1992.

OECD Development Assistance Committee (DAC). *Development cooperation report*, 1990 and 1991.

OECD Development Assistance Committee. *Twenty-five years of development cooperation*, Chairman's Report, 1985.

Oman, C. and Wignaraja, G. *The post-war evolution of development thinking*, OECD Development Centre, 1991.

Overseas Development Council. 'Debt reductions and North-South resource transfers to the year 2000', *Policy Essay No 3*, Washington DC, February 1992.

R. Cassen & Associates. Does aid work?, 1986.

Rostow, W. W. *The stages of economic growth: A non-communist manifesto*, 1960.

Rufin, J.-C. *L'empire et les nouveaux barbares*, Paris, 1991.

South Commission. *The challenge to the South*, 1990.

Turner, P. 'Capital flows in the 1980s: A survey of major trends', *BIS Economic Papers*, No 30, Basle, 1991.

Unctad. *Trade and development report*, 1991.

UNDP. Human development report, 1990, 1991 and 1992.

Unicef, (eds. Gomia, G. A., Jolly, R., Steward, F.), *Adjustment with a human face*, 1987.

United Nations. *World economic survey*, 1991.

United Nations. 'Preventive diplomacy, peacemaking and peacekeeping', report of the Secretary-General of the United Nations, June 1992.

Van Dam, F. 'Noord-Zuid balans van veertig jaar', *Internationale Spectator*, June 1992.

Von Verschuer, H. The future world economic order, 1991.

World Bank. *Managing development: The governance dimension*, 1991.

World Bank. *European integration and the developing world* (G. Pohl, P. Sorsa), 1992.

World Bank. *The impact of EC-92 on developing countries' trade: A dissenting view*, 1992.

World Bank. *Global economic prospects and the developing countries*, reports, 1991, 1992 and 1993.

World Bank. *Social dimensions of adjustments*, report, 1987.

World Bank. *Sub-Saharan Africa – from crisis to sustainable growth: A long-term prospective study*, report, 1989.

World Bank. *World development report, 1990* ('Poverty'), 1991 ('The challenge of development') and 1992 ('Development and the environment').

World Commission on Environment and Development. *Our common future*, Brundtland report, 1987.

World Resources 1992–93 – Towards sustainable development – A guide to the global environment, 1992.

World Watch Institute. *State of the world*, Reports, 1991 and 1992.

The Forward Studies Unit

The Forward Studies Unit was set up in 1989 as a department of the European Commission reporting directly to the President.

It consists of a multicultural, multidisciplinary team of some 15 members who are responsible for monitoring the forward march of European integration while identifying structural trends and long-term prospects.

The Commission decision setting the unit up gave it three tasks:

- to monitor and evaluate European integration to 1992 and beyond;
- to establish permanent relations with national bodies involved in forecasting;
- to work in specific briefs.

The Forward Studies Unit has, to date, produced wide-ranging reports on new issues which, as a result, have frequently found their way into the mainstream of the Commission's work, developing a house style which applies a research method designed to bring out the diversity of Europe (Shaping Factors, Shaping Actors), developing an all-round and/or long-term view which makes it easier to secure consensus above and beyond particular national interests, keeping a watching brief on and an ear open to movements in Europe's societies by setting up links with research and forward studies institutions, and holding regular seminars on specific themes which are attended by prominent figures from the arts, the cultural sphere and universities and representatives of civil society, together with the President or a Member of the European Commission.

The futurological function has gradually developed outside the Unit, within several of the Commission's Directorates-General which are keen to adopt a strategic approach. The Unit serves as a point where all the various future-oriented think-tanks inside the Commission can meet together.

For some years now, the need for a forecasting function having grown as the work of the European Union has become wider and more complex, the work programme for the Forward Studies Unit has been updated each year so that it can be reoriented to meet specific needs and towards maximum cooperation with all the Commission departments concerned.

Information about the Unit's current work is available in the quarterly newsletter *Lettre des Carrefours* and on an Internet site.

Other titles published in this series

Shaping Actors, Shaping Factors in Russia's Future

The Mediterranean Society: A Challenge for Islam, Judaism and Christianity

Towards a More Coherent Global Economic Order